3,95

Expository Sermons on the Book of

Daniel

Volume 3 CHAPTERS IV - VI

BOOKS BY DR. CRISWELL . . .

Expository Sermons on the Book of

Daniel

Volume 3   Chapters IV - VI

W.A.Criswell

ZONDERVAN PUBLISHING HOUSE
GRAND RAPIDS, MICHIGAN

Expository Sermons on the Book of Daniel, Volume 3
© 1971 by Zondervan Publishing House
Grand Rapids, Michigan

Library of Congress Catalog Card Number 68-27468

Printed in the United States of America

CONTENTS

FOREWORD

God blessed to the hearts of His people the series of sermons published in this third volume on Daniel beyond any series I have ever preached during the twenty-seven years I have been pastor of our church here in Dallas. The interest in and the response to every message was an encouragement to my soul.

As I reread the typed messages, I see a great deal of repetition in the development of the background of the sermons. There is an obvious reason for this. The book was not written as one would sit down at a desk, where he would start at the first chapter and write to the concluding word. Rather, the sermons were prepared and preached to a living audience, and the words, recorded on tape, were transcribed on paper. This means that the congregation listening to the sermon had to be instructed in every instance in the context of the passage being expounded. Often many weeks separated the sermons — vacations, special events at the church, assignments on mission fields, revivals — and when this occurred the story of the text of necessity had to be reintroduced.

I once read a review of a book of expository sermons I had preached, published by Zondervan Publishing House. The reviewer made the comment that there was much repetition in the messages. The reason is the obvious one I have just stated in the paragraph above. Under God (serving Him first) the primary obligation of the preacher is to his congregation. Whatever helps them to understand the message is what the preacher ought to present. If that means repetition, then one must use repetition.

My deepest gratitude is hereby expressed to Dr. James Bryant, our assistant pastor at the First Baptist Church in Dallas, for his help in transcribing the sermons through his secretarial staff and for his gracious willingness to prepare them for publication. I would also like to thank Mrs. M. O. Lively, our church librarian, for her invaluable assistance in searching through hundreds of volumes to locate for me much needed and hard-to-find factual material. Nor would I forget to thank our loving Savior for the people who so earnestly pray for me in this ministry of preaching, without whose prayers the messages would be denied their saving power in reaching the lost and encouraging the saved.

Now may God bless you, dear reader, as you follow with me the life of the statesman-prophet, Daniel. The preparation and delivery of the sermons meant so much to me. May they mean as much to you.

W. A. Criswell

First Baptist Church
Dallas, Texas

THE REFINER'S FIRE

He sat by a furnace of sevenfold heat,
    As He watched by the precious ore;
And closer He bent, with a searching gaze,
    As He heated it more and more.

He knew He had ore that could stand the test;
    And He wanted the finest of gold —
To mould as a crown for the king to wear,
    Set with gems of a price untold.

So He laid our gold in the burning fire,
    Though we fain would have said Him nay;
And He watched the dross that we had not seen,
    As it melted and passed away.

And the gold grew brighter, and yet more bright;
    But our eyes were so dim with tears,
We saw but the fire — not the Master's hand,
    And questioned with anxious fears.

Yet our gold shone out with a richer glow,
    As it mirrored a form above
That bent o'er the fire — though unseen by us —
    With looks of ineffable love.

Can we think that it pleases His loving heart
    To cause us a moment's pain?
Ah! no, but He saw through the present loss
    The bliss of eternal gain.

So He waited there with a watchful eye,
    With a love that is strong and sure;
And His gold did not suffer a whit more heat
    Than was needed to make it pure.

— Author Unknown

From *Sourcebook of Poetry*, compiled by Al Bryant, pp. 681-682.
Copyright, 1968, by Zondervan Publishing House, Grand Rapids,
Michigan.

LYCANTHROPY

Chapter 1

LYCANTHROPY

Nebuchadnezzar the king, unto all people, nations, and languages, that dwell in all the earth; Peace be multiplied unto you.

I thought it good to shew the signs and wonders that the high God hath wrought toward me.

How great are his signs! and how mighty are his wonders! his kingdom is an everlasting kingdom, and his dominion is from generation to generation.

I Nebuchadnezzar was at rest in mine house, and flourishing in my palace:

I saw a dream which made me afraid, and the thoughts upon my bed and the visions of my head troubled me.

Therefore made I a decree to bring in all the wise men of Babylon before me, that they might make known unto me the interpretation of the dream.

Then came in the magicians, the astrologers, the Chaldeans, and the soothsayers: and I told the dream before them; but they did not make known unto me the interpretation thereof.

But at the last Daniel came in before me, whose name was Belteshazzar, according to the name of my god, and in whom is the spirit of the holy gods: and before him I told the dream, saying,

O Belteshazzar, master of the magicians, because I know that the spirit of the holy gods is in thee, and no secret troubleth thee, tell me the visions of my dream that I have seen, and the interpretation thereof.

Thus were the visions of mine head in my bed; I

saw, and behold a tree in the midst of the earth, and the height thereof was great.

The tree grew, and was strong, and the height thereof reached unto heaven, and the sight thereof to the end of all the earth:

The leaves thereof were fair, and the fruit thereof much, and in it was meat for all: the beasts of the field had shadow under it, and the fowls of the heaven dwelt in the boughs thereof, and all flesh was fed of it.

I saw in the visions of my head upon my bed, and, behold, a watcher and an holy one came down from heaven;

He cried aloud, and said thus, Hew down the tree, and cut off his branches, shake off his leaves, and scatter his fruit: let the beasts get away from under it, and the fowls from his branches:

Nevertheless leave the stump of his roots in the earth, even with a band of iron and brass, in the tender grass of the field; and let it be wet with the dew of heaven, and let his portion be with the beasts in the grass of the earth:

Let his heart be changed from man's, and let a beast's heart be given unto him; and let seven times pass over him.

This matter is by the decree of the watchers, and the demand by the word of the holy ones: to the intent that the living may know that the most High ruleth in the kingdom of men, and giveth it to whomsoever he will, and setteth up over it the basest of men.

This dream I king Nebuchadnezzar have seen. Now thou, O Belteshazzar, declare the interpretation thereof, forasmuch as all the wise men of my kingdom are not able to make known unto me the interpretation: but thou art able; for the spirit of the holy gods is in thee.

Then Daniel, whose name was Belteshazzar, was astonied for one hour, and his thoughts troubled him. The king spake, and said, Belteshazzar, let not the dream, or the interpretation thereof, trouble thee. Belteshazzar answered and said, My Lord, the dream be to them that hate thee, and the interpretation thereof to thine enemies.

The tree that thou sawest, which grew, and was strong, whose height reached unto the heaven, and the sight thereof to all the earth;

Whose leaves were fair, and the fruit thereof much, and in it was meat for all; under which the beasts of the field dwelt, and upon whose branches the fowls of the heaven had their habitation:

It is thou, O king, that art grown and become strong: for thy greatness is grown, and reacheth unto heaven, and thy dominion to the end of the earth.

And whereas the king saw a watcher and an holy one coming down from heaven, and saying, Hew the tree down, and destroy it; yet leave the stump of the roots thereof in the earth, even with a band of iron and brass, in the tender grass of the field; and let it be wet with the dew of heaven, and let his portion be with the beasts of the field, till seven times pass over him;

This is the interpretation, O king, and this is the decree of the most High, which is come upon my lord the king:

That they shall drive thee from men, and thy dwelling shall be with the beasts of the field, and they shall make thee to eat grass as oxen, and they shall wet thee with the dew of heaven, and seven times shall pass over thee, till thou know that the most High ruleth in the kingdom of men, and giveth it to whomsoever he will.

And whereas they commanded to leave the stump of the tree roots; thy kingdom shall be sure unto thee, after that thou shalt have known that the heavens do rule.

Wherefore, O king, let my counsel be acceptable unto thee, and break off thy sins by righteousness, and thine iniquities by shewing mercy to the poor; if it may be a lengthening of thy tranquillity.

All this came upon the king Nebuchadnezzar.

At the end of twelve months he walked in the palace of the kingdom of Babylon.

The king spake, and said, Is not this great Babylon, that I have built for the house of the kingdom by the might of my power, and for the honour of my majesty?

While the word was in the king's mouth, there fell a voice from heaven, saying, O king Nebuchadnezzar, to thee it is spoken; The kingdom is departed from thee.

And they shall drive thee from men, and thy dwelling shall be with the beasts of the field: they shall make thee to eat grass as oxen, and seven times shall pass over thee, until thou know that the most High ruleth in the kingdom of men, and giveth it to whomsoever he will.

The same hour was the thing fulfilled upon Nebuchadnezzar: and he was driven from men, and did eat grass as oxen, and his body was wet with the dew of heaven, till his hairs were grown like eagles' feathers, and his nails like birds' claws.

Daniel 4:1-33

This chapter in Daniel is a tract that King Nebuchadnezzar wrote through Daniel. It contains Nebuchadnezzar's heathen expressions and ideas, as well as his experience in coming to the true God. It is a tract describing his conversion. In his testimony he presents an unusual experience: a judgment of God upon his sins called "lycanthropy." "Lycanthropy" is a term that describes a man who, afflicted with monomania, thinks of himself as an animal. Out of that dramatic experience came Nebuchadnezzar's conversion to the true God. He writes the tract in Aramaic and addresses it to all inhabitants of the earth.

THE MERCY OF GOD

First, we have in this passage an illustration of the long-suffering and mercy of God to a cruel, heathen king. The king is not a member of the covenant family of Israel. He is a heathen, which brings to us the knowledge that God is not only the God of Israel, but He is also the God of all the families, kingdoms, and nations of the earth. This great king begins his address, "Nebuchadnezzar the king, unto all people, nations, and languages, that dwell in all the earth" (4:1). The mercy of God is not confined to the nation of Israel. God's goodness reaches out to all the nations of the earth. We have a marvelous demonstration of that goodness in God's mercy toward Nineveh. He sent a prophet (Jonah) to heathen Assyria to proclaim the mercies of and to demonstrate the salvation of the Lord. Now God is going to do it again in Babylon.

Nebuchadnezzar is the first great king of the times of the Gentiles. He is that "golden head" of the giant image of world history described in Daniel 2. We are deeply interested in him. When Nebuchadnezzar talks, how does he talk? What does he say? How does this infantile giant describe his new-found faith? It will do our souls good to listen to him.

As Nebuchadnezzar begins his word of testimony, he is baffled and overwhelmed by the glory of Jehovah God. "I thought it good to shew the signs and wonders that the high God hath wrought toward me" (4:2). Then you would expect him to tell you all about the signs and wonders. But floods of overwhelming glory fill his soul, and what he says is just exclamation. "How great are his signs! and how mighty are his wonders!" (4:3). We find that same overwhelming inability to describe religious experience in the apostle Paul. After Paul struggles through Romans 9, 10 and 11 to describe the sovereignty and the elective purposes of God, he just ends in an exclamation. He cannot say more. "O the depth of the riches both of the wisdom and knowledge of God! how unsearchable are his judgments, and his ways past finding out!" (Rom. 11:33). This is true of any and all real religion. There is mystery in religion.

There is also infinitude. When a fellow stands up and says, "I'm going to tell it to you like it is," he has his God cornered in a small room. His religion is compartmentalized, it is outlined and here it is. He has God locked up in theology and in a book on a shelf. Anytime he wants the book, he just takes it down from the shelf and reads it. There is God. As though God can be contained in a book! Why, the heaven of the heavens cannot contain Him. No man can accurately and definitely place in words and syllables his religious experience. It goes beyond us. We are reaching out toward the inexpressible and the infinitude of the Almighty. Sometimes our creed can be expressed only in tears and sometimes our prayers can be said only in agonies of the soul. That is what Nebuchadnezzar found when he sought to describe the glorious experience of his confrontation with God. He just burst into exclamations. The glory overwhelmed his soul. After all, would it not be tragic if all there was to religion was cold, correct theology? Our souls would cry out against the assumption that all there is to this life are the logic and the reason by which we can understand it; as though there were nothing over and beyond what our finite minds can encompass. Many are persuaded that the essence of life can be placed in a test tube, and reduced to mathematical formulae. That is a tragedy. The Almighty placed in our souls a hunger for the infinite and gave us life to grasp the heavens, yet we propose to feed it on a handful of moondust. As though life could be defined and delineated in terms of scientific, physical, mathematical discovery! Ah, there's a wonder beyond. There is a glory beyond. True religion has to do with the infinite God and a mere man cannot describe the confrontation. You cannot put religion in mere human speech. The speech will not bear it.

After his exclamations, the king describes the great vision he had of the towering tree. "I Nebuchadnezzar was at rest in mine house, and flourishing in my palace" (Dan. 4:4). His wars of conquest are over. No longer is he marching at the head of his great army, subduing the entire civilized world. He is at rest. All of his enemies on the outside have been subdued, and all of his fears on the inside have been allayed. It is a complete and a full tranquillity which he enjoys. "At rest." Every goblet is full of wine. The corner of every one of his palaces is filled with music. Every room in all of his vast, richly furnished mansion is an escape and a refuge from the trials of this world. He lays his head on a downy pillow, there to dream of the luxury, the wealth, and the splendor of his golden dominion. "I was at rest in mine house, flourishing in my palace." Those great fortifications of Babylon and that mighty army of the Chaldean host stand ready to defend him at the blast of a trumpet. He is at rest.

THE STRANGE DREAM

In the midst of that rest, "I saw a dream which made me afraid" (4:5). Let us not tamper with the language. Leave it just as he wrote: "I saw a dream." It was a part of him, and yet he stood as someone outside and looked at it. "I saw a dream and it made me afraid." What! Nebuchadnezzar afraid? Why, he was the ruler of all the inhabitants then on earth. Afraid! Is not that just like God? He reaches into His bag of terrors and what things God can pull out of it! Nebuchadnezzar is afraid. This mighty monarch who conquered the civilized world, who is in his palace, who is behind impregnable fortifications, who is behind strong walls which were the wonder of the world, who is guarded by a mighty army — is afraid!

What things God can send! He reaches into His bag of terrors and He sends lightning and the awesome whirlwind. But we can build great, granite masonry walls to circumvent these disasters. God can reach in His bag and send an earthquake. But we can erect buildings that move with the earth tremors. He can reach in that bag and send fire. But we can make things incombustible. Then the Lord God reaches into the bag of terrors and He sends a dream. How do you build fortifications against a dream? How do you make war against a vision? A dream! "I saw a dream and was afraid." This great monarch is a cowering knave. He is afraid of a dream.

Is it not strange how God, back in that day before the prophecy was completed, spoke to those people? A dream! He spoke to Abimelech in a dream. He spoke to Pharaoh's butler and baker in a dream. He spoke to Pharaoh, himself, in a dream. Do you remember Gideon? God sent him to the Midianite camp to listen to a Midianite who had a dream about a barley loaf which had overthrown his whole army. Do you remember Pontius Pilate sitting in judgment on Christ? His wife sent him word and said: "I had a dream tonight. I had a dream about that man and I have suffered" (Matt. 27:19).

In the dream, Nebuchadnezzar saw a great towering tree, a mighty tree that could be seen from the ends of the earth. And the tree grew and grew. It was an awesome sight. Often the tree of paradise can be seen in Assyrian and Babylonian culture. The people carved it on gems, on ornaments, and on great buildings. It was seen everywhere and signified the power and the regal authority of the monarch himself. The description of the vision continued: "The leaves of the tree were fair, and the fruit of the tree was multiplied. And under the shadow of it the beast and animals of the earth did find refuge. And while I was looking, a watcher and a Holy One from heaven" (now Nebuchadnezzar is talking in his Babylonian language of mythology), "said, 'Cut it down. Cut off its branches. Shake off its leaves and scatter its fruit.' And the great tree was hewed down, utterly destroyed. But the stump was left and a band of brass and iron was placed around it to protect it." Cut down a cedar tree, and it will never grow back. Cut down a cypress tree, and it will never grow back. Cut down a fir tree, and it will never grow back. But most trees have a shoot from the stump. Leave that stump and guard it (as here with a band of brass and iron) and the tree will revive to grow again. Then in the vision the language of Scripture changes from "it" to "he" in speaking of the stump. "And let seven times (seven years) pass over it and let a beast heart be given it until *he* knows that God is God." That is the dream.

The king sent for his college of counselors, magicians, astrologers, and the Chaldean hierarchy of priests, but they had no idea what the dream meant. Last of all, that is, when these subordinates could not answer the question, the king sent for Daniel, his great and golden counselor. He told the dream to Daniel and when Daniel heard it he was "astonied" for an hour. "Astonied." That is an archaic word; it means "speechless." Daniel's countenance was altered and he sat terrified before the king. Thereupon the king said: "Don't be terrified, Daniel, but speak. What does the dream mean?"

Now what do you do? There is no preacher who ever lived, there is no messenger from God who ever spoke for Him, and there is no apostle or prophet who was ever sent to bear tidings from heaven, but who faces that dilemma. What shall he say? For if he delivers the truth, he is pronouncing the doom of a man's life. What shall he say?

What Shall the Preacher Say

When Paul stood before Felix and Drusilla, that abominable, unspeakable pair, he could have pondered the alternative. "Shall I reason of righteousness and temperance and judgment to come, or shall I palliate and compliment and be sycophantic? What shall I do?" When the man of God stands before stiff-necked, recalcitrant people, shall he say words of truth? What shall he do? Shall the preacher tell the people the truth of God or shall he not? My observation is that the average preacher does not do it. Rather, he fills the pit of hell and damnation with flowers. He speaks to compliment. It is not popular to denounce sin and to threaten men with what God says about judgment to come. So we empty the Bible of its penal words. We say to a half-damned man: "Let it not trouble you. Judgment will not fall. Why, someday you will be taken to heaven no matter what you do and someday you will be one of the seraphim, or at least an angel."

What shall the preacher do? Why do not we do as Daniel? He stood in front of the king as a slave. By the power of the king his life could be snuffed out. He stood in the presence of the king where there was a den of lions waiting, where there was a fiery furnace waiting. Daniel stood in the presence of the king and delivered faithfully God's message, "It is thou, O king." Does that remind you of anything? Is not that what Nathan, the true prophet of God, said to David? "Thou art the man." Is not that what Stephen said in the presence of the Sanhedrin? That is what Daniel said in the presence of the king, "It is thou, O king." Then he delivered the message. What a message! A message about lycanthropy.

The Beast Heart

For seven years the king shall be insane, a madman. He shall think of himself as an animal and shall act like it. He shall be a monomaniac; that is, in just that one area of his life will he be demented and deranged. He will be perfectly all right except he will think he is an animal. In all the areas of his life he will have his entire faculties, except in that one. And for seven years will he live that horrible, deranged insanity. He is to have the heart of a beast and he is to act like it.

Now I want to discuss that. "Lycanthropy" is a malady,

a disease, an aberration which has been known through the centuries. Is not that a strange thing? Sometimes you will hear discussions of it under the term "boanthropy." "Bos" is the Latin word for "cow" or "bull" and "anthropos" is the Greek word for "man." The man feels that he is a cow or an ox and acts like it. Sometimes you will run across the word "avianthropy." "Avis" is the Latin word for "bird" and "anthropos" is the Greek word for "man." "Avianthropy." The fellow thinks that he is a bird. In my studying this week I came across an instance where a man thought he was a cock pheasant, and he roosted in a tree every night instead of sleeping in a bed! "Avianthropy." But the word usually used to include all of those psychological aberrations and delusions is "lycanthropy." The insanity is most modern. It is most ancient. While I was preparing and preaching this sermon a funny article came out in *The Dallas Morning News*, written on the front page by the feature columnist Paul Crume. Here is what he wrote:

> Sid Moore is an old Navy hand who has recently joined the Department of Agriculture to do whatever a public information type can do to stamp out hog cholera.
>
> He was in Texas recently to help set up a cholera headquarters in Waco, a reflection of Texas' status as the number one hot spot at present. Moore's job is not always that simple, however. He was doing a similar job last fall in Virginia and North Carolina, and on his third day on the job he took a telephone call from a county agent.
>
> The county agent confessed to a problem. A newspaperman had telephoned him and asked whether it was true that a 17-year-old boy in his town, a high school football star, was under a doctor's care for treatment of hog cholera.
>
> "Impossible," the county agency had replied, "hog cholera affects swine. It doesn't have anything to do with the cholera that people have."
>
> *Still, the area was under hog cholera quarantine, and the county agent had thought he ought to report the incident.*

MOORE'S BOSSES thought they had better check the story out too. They instructed their head veterinarian to call the boy's family physician.

The doctor apologized and said the story was all his fault. He had, he said, been trying only to humor the boy's father.

The doctor added that the boy's father had conceived the unusual idea that he had somehow turned into a boar hog and that, as a boar, he had come down with the hog cholera and passed it on to his son.

"Actually," said the doctor, "I have been treating the boy for a simple case of poison ivy."

"My — ," exclaimed the veterinarian, after more than the proper amount of stunned silence. "Is this man running loose in the community?"

"I hope to tell you he is," replied the doctor. "He is our local commonwealth attorney."

The stunned silence this time lasted almost an eternity.

"But don't worry," the doctor finally said. "The whole community knows about the father's peculiarities, and the newspaper is not likely to print the story."

The newspaper didn't, and Moore became aware that the Lord sometimes interferes even on the side of flacks.

Lycanthropy is a strange malady, indeed! When we look at the word itself, "lycanthropy" is made up of the Greek word "lukos" meaning "wolf" and "anthropos" meaning "man." Lycanthropy technically would, therefore, refer to a man who thinks of himself as a wolf.

Long ago the power of transforming others into wild beasts was attributed not only to malignant sorcerers, but also to Christian saints. A Russian story tells how Peter and Paul turned an impious husband and wife into bears. St. Patrick, of Ireland, was said to have transformed Vereticus, king of Wales, into a wolf. And St. Natalis cursed an illustrious Irish family with the result that each member of it was doomed to be a wolf for seven years. The fearful aberration also enters into the tradition of Europe, especially in legends of the werewolf. Either by curse or by choice, a man could turn himself into a wolf and then eat human flesh and drink human blood. Such a man was a werewolf and hid in dens. In our own American culture we have the tradition of "beauty and the beast." I have seen movies advertised with a frightful beast holding a beautiful girl in his arms. That tradition is common in the cultural life of all humanity. And it comes from this disease, from this psychological illusion called "lycanthropy." King Nebuchadnezzar was to be turned into a beast, insane for seven years.

It is not unusual for a king to be insane. Many kings have been schizophrenic. They were one thing one day and another thing another day. The madness of kings is a part of history. One example is Charles VI of France. Another is Christian VII of Denmark. Still another is George III of England. Another is the mad king of Bavaria. You can write books on the madness of kings. And this is the judgment of God upon Nebuchadnezzar, "lycanthropy." "And it will continue," says the prophet, "until you get right, until you acknowledge the true God of all the heavens."

The Prophet's Appeal

But the prophet made an appeal. Daniel had an affection for that heathen king which shows itself over and over again. Daniel makes an appeal. "Wherefore, O King," he says, "let my counsel be acceptable unto thee." He talks like a true courtier. "O king, let my counsel be acceptable unto thee. Break off thy sins by righteousness, and thine iniquities by shewing mercy to the poor; if it may be a lengthening of thy tranquillity."

Look at the great theological implications of that appeal on the part of the prophet Daniel. The decree is not "kismet." It is not fate. This world is not run by fate. It is run by God. There is nothing ultimately impersonal in it. It is God who superintends and supervises. And it is His sovereignty which guides and decrees. "Nebuchadnezzar, if you will break off your sins, if you will repent, if you will turn from your iniquities — God is a loving God and a forgiving God and He will abate the fearful judgment." Is not that the truth of the Book? There are no final decrees of damnation from the Lord God Almighty on this side of eternity. If man will turn, God will turn. If a man will change, God will change. If a man will repent, God will repent.

The Lord God sent Jonah to Nineveh with this thundering, burning message, "Forty days and Nineveh shall be destroyed." The Lord God looked down from heaven and saw the king of Nineveh sitting in sackcloth and ashes. He further saw the nobles of Nineveh in contrition and repentance. Then he saw the whole city, crying for mercy. What did the Lord do? The Lord changed His mind. What He said he would do, He did not do. When Nineveh changed, God changed. When Nineveh got right, the Lord showed Himself a God of mercy. That is the Book. When God says, "Thou shalt surely die," if a man will repent and obey the Lord, he will live. When God says that there is damnation and judgment, God also says, "If you will turn, you will be forgiven."

THE KING'S PROBATION

God gave Nebuchadnezzar a probation of twelve months. God never executes a sentence immediately, swiftly. He warns, He decries, He delineates, He pleads, and He begs. He never executes a sentence swiftly. Always there is that period of probation. For Nebuchadnezzar it was twelve months.

In the days of the flood God said, "I will destroy the

world." A hundred and twenty years later, not immediately, but 120 years later that destruction came to pass. Noah, the preacher of righteousness, preached 120 years without a convert. Can you imagine a man doing that? Can you imagine my standing in this pulpit preaching 120 years and not a single person ever turning to God? That is the way it was in Noah's day. Yet God gave 120 years probation, giving the people an opportunity to turn. That is the Lord.

Of Hophni and Phinehas, those evil sons of Eli the high priest, God said, "Eli, if you do not change, if you do not correct those boys, I will destroy your house forever." In the second chapter of I Samuel it is recorded that God sent a prophet to warn Eli, and the whole chapter is taken up in that warning. In the third chapter God raised up little Samuel to warn Eli. Yet Eli did not change and the judgment finally fell.

The Lord God said to Samuel when he was mourning over Saul: "I have given him years and years to repent and change. Now I have rejected him." The Lord God said to Solomon, "All of these marvelous endowments will I give you, and besides that I will add length of life if you will obey Me." He gave Solomon many glorious gifts, but the Lord finally cut him down because of his disobedience. By the Spirit of the Lord Jeremiah cried to wicked Judah, "Repent." They refused to repent and in judgment Nebuchadnezzar came in 605 B.C. Jeremiah lifted up his voice again and said, "Repent, get right with God." Nebuchadnezzar in judgment came back in 598 B.C. Jeremiah lifted up his voice again and said, "Repent, get right with God." But they would not. For the third time Nebuchadnezzar came as the rod of God's anger and the staff of His indignation in 587 B.C. He did not need to come again. He plowed Jerusalem up and carried the people into captivity. God always gives that period of probation. He does not execute the sentence swiftly, but He will eventually and finally do so. That is why Proverbs 29:1 says, "He, that being often reproved hardeneth his neck, shall suddenly be destroyed, and that without remedy." Finally, the unrepentant sinner shall be destroyed and that without recourse of appeal.

That is why the Holy Spirit pleads with men today, "If you will hear His voice, do not harden your heart." God never pleads tomorrow, but right now, today. That is why the Apostle Paul quoted words of the Lord God when he said, "We . . . beseech you also that ye receive not the grace of God in vain. (For he saith, I have heard thee in a time accepted, and in the day of salvation have I succoured thee: behold, now is the accepted time; behold, now is the day of salvation") (II Cor. 6:1, 2). If God looks down from heaven (and He does), then that same Lord God says to you today, "If you will come, I will come. If you will walk down that aisle, I will meet you. If you will open your heart, I will come in. If you will look to heaven, I will answer. If you will give Me your life, I will take care of it like a deposit. If you will trust Me, I will see you through." That is the Lord pleading with you to come. And when a man answers with his life, God is there to see him through. God pleads with you today as Daniel pled with the king. Turn in humility and faith to Jesus. Acknowledge your utter dependence on Him. Already God's judgment has been pronounced. The warning has been given. But if you will turn to Jesus, God will turn that judgment away from you. He stands ready and willing to forgive and to save. Are you ready to come in repentance and in faith to Him?

Light Shining Out of Darkness

God moves in a mysterious way
 His wonders to perform;
He plants his footsteps in the sea
 And rides upon the storm.

Deep in unfathomable mines
 Of never-failing skill,
He treasures up His bright designs
 And works His sovereign will.

Ye fearful saints, fresh courage take;
 The clouds ye so much dread
Are big with mercy and shall break
 In blessings on your head.

Judge not the Lord by feeble sense,
 But trust Him for His grace;
Behind a frowning providence
 He hides a smiling face.

His purposes will ripen fast,
 Unfolding every hour;
The bud may have a bitter taste,
 But sweet will be the flower.

Blind unbelief is sure to err
 And scan His work in vain;
God is His own Interpreter
 And He will make it plain.

     — *William Cowper*

Chapter 2

THE BEAST HEART

THE BEAST HEART

The same hour was the thing fulfilled upon Nebuchadnezzar: and he was driven from men, and did eat grass
as oxen, and his body was wet with the dew of heaven,
till his hairs were grown like eagles' feathers, and his
nails like birds' claws.   Daniel 4:33

INTRODUCTORY

Several people have said to me: "You say that the fourth
chapter of the Book of Daniel is a tract. It is a personal
testimony written by Nebuchadnezzar through Daniel. If
that is true," they ask, "how is it that you say the Bible is
the inspired, inerrant Word of God, when this is a tract
written by a heathen king?" We must understand what is
meant by the inerrant, infallible, inspired Word of God. The
inspiration, the infallibility, the inerrancy lies in the truth of
the record. It is written here in the Bible just as it happened.

In the Holy Scriptures Satan speaks, but his words are
truthfully and inerrantly recorded. In the Bible are listed
long pages of what Job's comforters said. They were like
cactus plants and cockleburs, but their thorny words are
written here in the Bible. In the Bible you have the words
of false prophets, false witnesses, and false apostles. The
biblical inerrancy lies in the truth of the record. It is here

in the Bible exactly as it happened. When I read the Bible, I am reading the truth of the record. So in the fourth chapter of the book of Daniel we have a tract written by a heathen king and it happened exactly as it is recorded here in the immutable, infallible Word of God. This is exactly what that king said.

The King's Confrontation With God

The title of the message today, "The Beast Heart," is taken from Daniel 4:33: "The same hour was the thing fulfilled upon Nebuchadnezzar: and he was driven from men, and did eat grass as oxen, and his body was wet with the dew of heaven, till his hairs were grown like eagles' feathers, and his nails like birds' claws." The chapter begins with the king being at rest in his palace in Babylon. His wars of conquest are done. He is now consolidating his world authority and building his golden city. And as he lies at rest, you would think he would dream dreams of affluence, wealth, splendor and grandeur, but instead, he dreams a dream which frightens him. In the dream he sees a tall, towering, terrible tree which is cut down. When Daniel finally is invited to interpret the dream, the dream is seen as a message from God to Nebuchadnezzar. It is a message which bears a rod of smiting and correction. Nebuchadnezzar will be insane for seven years. He will be a madman until he repents, bows in acknowledgment of his sins, turns from them, and receives the most high God as the true Lord of all the earth.

Now, the decrees of God, as He threatens men with judgment, are always conditional. The universe seems to run by mechanical laws and motions. Actually, this is not so. The universe is controlled by a personal God. Always in God's judgmental warnings, there is a way of escape, if we will but seek it. So, when Daniel delivers that message of awesome judgment to King Nebuchadnezzar, he closes with an appeal. "Wherefore, O king, let my counsel be acceptable unto thee." As graciously and as sweetly as a courtier who bows before his monarch, does Daniel plead with Nebuchadnezzar. "Wherefore, O king, let my counsel be acceptable unto thee, and break off thy sins by righteousness, and thine iniquities by shewing mercy to the poor; if it may be a lengthening of thy tranquillity." Why this awesome judgment upon Nebuchadnezzar? Seven years to be insane and to live like a beast! Why that awesome judgment upon Nebuchadnezzar? There are several answers.

God's Judgment Justified

First, Nebuchadnezzar was a personally cruel and tempestuously violent man. He had no self-restraint in his anger. Every conquest but added to his arrogance and vanity. He was cruel beyond even what oriental monarchs are and have been known to be. For example, in the book of Daniel, in the second chapter, the king is preparing to butcher an entire class of men simply because *they* could not recall to him a dream which *he* had forgotten. In the third chapter of the book the king is seen heating a furnace seven times hotter than was usual for the roasting of three Hebrew young men who refused to bow down before his golden image. In Jeremiah 29 the prophet names two Jews whom Nebuchadnezzar roasted in fire. In II Kings 25 Nebuchadnezzar put out King Zedekiah's eyes after he had slain the man's sons before his face. The last thing Zedekiah ever saw was the death of his sons. In II Kings 24 Nebuchadnezzar takes Jehoiakim, who is only eighteen years of age, and imprisons him thirty-six years for an offense. Nebuchadnezzar personally was cruel, violent, tempestuous, and fiercely vindictive.

Second, politically, Nebuchadnezzar brought untold misery to the world. Not content with laying under tribute the nations which he conquered, the king pursued the bitter practice of the cruel Assyrian. He uprooted the people, deported whole nations, and resettled them as strangers in a strange land. Think of the hopelessness, the helplessness and the untold, indescribable misery of whole peoples as they were deported from their homes and carried way into a foreign country. Why, the path of the victor's march could be marked by the corpses of women, children, the old, and the sick who were not able to keep pace with the army. And think of those people as they lifted up their eyes to see their homes gone, their nation destroyed, and themselves living in a strange land. One can feel the heartthrob, the blood drops, and the tears of Psalm 137: "By the rivers (by the canals) of Babylon, there we sat down, yea, we wept, when we remembered Zion. We hanged our harps upon the willows in the midst thereof. For there they that carried us away captive required of us a song; and they that wasted us required of us mirth, saying, Sing us one of the songs of Zion." How do you sing the Lord's song in a strange land?

Not only was Nebuchadnezzar personally cruel and vindictive, not only was he militarily and politically indifferent to the cries of the helpless people, but he was also arrogant and proud. When Daniel said to him, "Thou art that golden head," Nebuchadnezzar coveted the entire image to be of himself and to be made out of solid gold. In the third chapter of this book, Nebuchadnezzar sets himself above even his gods. If one of his gods displeased him, the king would burn the priest and raze the temple to the ground.

Why the judgment of God upon Nebuchadnezzar? He refused to repent. Nebuchadnezzar, the king, in his authority and grandeur, had a courtier and that courtier, Daniel, bowed before him and said: "O king, let my counsel be acceptable unto thee, and break off thy sins by righteousness, and thine iniquities by shewing mercy to the poor." Did he do it? No. Though he was eminently and preeminently successful, the greatest general who possibly ever marched at the head of a conquering army, righteousness was no part of his program. The prophet, Habakkuk, describes in prophetic prediction the coming of the army of Nebuchadnezzar. "Lo, I raise up the Chaldeans, that bitter and hasty nation, which shall march through the breadth of the land. . . . They are terrible and dreadful. . . . Their horses are swifter than the leopards, and are more fierce than the evening wolves . . . They shall come all for violence: their faces shall sup up as the east wind and they shall gather the captivity as the sand" (Hab. 1:6-9). Righteousness? Nebuchadnezzar did not know the meaning of the word nor did he propose to learn it. And as for mercy — Break off "thine iniquities by shewing mercy to the poor" — I do not know whether he ever heard the word or not. To us it is second nature to think of the desperation and despair of the poor. But to Nebuchadnezzar, like Napoleon, the poor were canon fodder. And as for his golden city, he was building it with slave labor. He populated his empire around Chaldean Babylon with those miserable, unhappy wretches, whom he dispossessed from their home land and brought to be his slaves. Mercy? Whoever heard that the poor had rights? Mercy? Why, the poor were like animals to him. They were to be used simply for the furtherance of his own prideful ambition.

But the day of judgment fell at the end of twelve months. How earnestly did the Lord plead with him through Daniel. But by the end of twelve months, Nebuchadnezzar had forgotten it. The appeal of his servant and statesman Daniel had left the king's memory. For twelve months — ah! Nebuchadnezzar may have forgotten, but not God.

> Though the mills of God grind slowly
>   Yet they grind exceeding small;
> Though with patience He stands waiting,
>   With exactness grinds He all.

At the end of twelve months God's judgment fell. If a man will not listen to the quiet pleadings of the Lord, if he hardens his heart and closes his ears against the sweet whisperings of the Spirit of intercession, then the Lord has terrors in His hand for that man. He has damnations and judgments at His command. He has a smiting rod and a correcting staff. The judgments of God are awesome to behold. And to Nebuchadnezzar they came about like this.

GOD'S JUDGMENT FALLS

At the end of twelve months Nebuchadnezzar was walking on the top of his golden palace. Picture the king, proud, arrogant, the dictator of the whole civilized earth. The riches of the Mediterranean and the Persian Gulf, the Elamites, the Egyptians, the Armenians, the Syrians, the Jews, the whole earth was his — all of it. See him as he walked on the top of his golden palace, followed by his administrators, his lords, and his counselors. As he walked, they reverently, and at a distance, followed behind. When he came to the end of the terrace, he turned. And they obsequiously, sycophantly bowed on either side, and opened a way for him to walk in between. He did not mark their presence. He was not even mindful of them, for he was filled with pride and selfishness. The king spoke: "Is not this great Babylon?" See him look over the balustrade of his golden palace at the horizon of Babylon from sky to sky. It rises in splendor. "Is not this great Babylon, that *I* have built for the house of the kingdom by the might of *my* power and for the honour of *my* majesty?" Ah, every syllable of it describes the glory and pride of that arrogant monarch.

And just when he said it, like a clap of thunder, like an earthquake, like an intervention and interdiction from heaven, like lightning and fire, suddenly the king's mind snapped and he went insane. One moment, standing in grandeur and arrogance, the totalitarian monarch of the entire civilized world. His eyes were steady, his gaze was clear, his mind worked with the gifted genius of the golden head of that world image depicted in Daniel 2. But in the next moment his eye was unsteady. He had the countenance and furtive look of a beast. He was mad. As one full of fear, despair, and dismay, he hid himself. The king ran away from his fears. Like an ox, an animal, he hid himself in the thickets along the Euphrates River. The abashment was that dismal. It was complete and remorseless. This king, who as the general of his army, had conquered the whole earth, now hid in fear and desperation in the thickets, in the fields, in the forests, in the wilderness. This man who sat at the table, tasting all the dainties of the earth, now ate grass like an ox. He was a monomaniac. He had all of his faculties and emotions, except just one. He thought he was a beast. He had a beast heart. The horror of it, the agony of it, the distress of it lasted for seven long, interminable years.

FROM JUDGMENT TO MERCY

But at the end of the days, seven years, "I Nebuchadnezzar lifted up mine eyes unto heaven." What does that recall to you? Psalm 121 says: "I will lift up mine eyes unto the hills, from whence cometh my help. My help cometh from the Lord, which made heaven and earth." At the end of the days, "I Nebuchadnezzar lifted up mine eyes unto heaven." Does that recall to you the story of the prodigal son, who far from home, and in a far country and in a pig pen, came to himself? Does that bring to your mind the Gadarene demoniac whom Jesus healed and who was now sitting clothed, in his right mind, looking up into the face of Jesus? At the end of the days, "I Nebuchadnezzar lifted up mine eyes to heaven." He had turned. He had changed. He had repented. "And I blessed the most High, and I praised and honoured him that liveth for ever." He found the Lord!

Some men will not find Him any other way. They have to be beaten down. They have to be smitten under the rod of God's correction. They will not learn any other way. Under the awesome judgment, Nebuchadnezzar had finally raised his eyes to heaven, and blessed the most High God who liveth forever and ever. And is God merciful? He always is. When you change, He changes. When you turn, He turns. The smiting hand and the correcting rod become our staff, and our strength, and our blessing.

"And my reason returned unto me." When a man is outside of God, he is mad. When a man turns aside from the mercies of the Almighty, he is insane. He had lost his mind. But when a man is his best self, in his finest intellect, when a man has reached the zenith of his glory as a thinking, intelligent, moral creature, his reason has come back. He is thinking right. And he thinks about God. "My reason returned unto me; and for the glory of my kingdom, mine honour and brightness returned unto me; and my counselors and my lords sought unto me; and I was established in my kingdom, and excellent majesty was added unto me."

Why and how could it have been that that kingdom was maintained for Nebuchadnezzar for seven, interminable years, while he was mad? The fact is unbelievably extraordinary. Did you know that when Nebuchadnezzar died, his son, Evil-Merodach, who inherited the throne, reigned but three years? He was murdered to make room for a usurper. And did you know the Babylonian kingdom lasted only twenty-seven years after Nebuchadnezzar and then it was destroyed forever? It disappeared from the face of the earth. Yet, for seven long years the kingdom is maintained for Nebuchadnezzar. Would you not have thought that those nations which he had conquered would have re-

belled? Would you not have thought that those wild tribes
he held in subservience would have gone on pillage, ram-
page, and plunder? Would you not have thought his envious
son or an ambitious administrator would have seized the
throne? Yet, the kingdom is quiet. Why and how? I think,
for one thing, because of his wife, Amytis, the queen, the
Median mountain girl whom the king had married and on
whom he had lavished those unbelievable gifts of grandeur.
For her Nebuchadnezzar had raised a mountain called "The
hanging gardens," one of the seven wonders of the ancient
world. The queen must have had a part in preserving the
kingdom for Nebuchadnezzar.

But above all, and most of all, I think it was his faithful
visor, Daniel, who did it. He guided the affairs of the kingdom, keeping the promise of God before him, knowing that
at the end of those seven years, if Nebuchadnezzar humbled
himself, God would give him back his scepter and his throne
and his freedom. And known to Daniel was the exact day
ending those seven years. The great statesman-prophet and
faithful friend sought out the once mad monarch. Is not
that a strange thing? Daniel seemingly loved the king
despite the king's vindictive cruelty and his fierce, volatile
spirit. Daniel seemed to love him, and I can just see Daniel
at the head of the king's counselors, lords and governors. I
can see him at the head of the distinguished group, searching in a wilderness, in a forest, in a thicket. "My counsellors and my lords sought me." Led by Daniel, they finally
found the king in some deserted place. God had restored his
reason. He is the same glorious monarch who had conquered
the world and built the golden city and kingdom of Babylon,
except for one thing. The old arrogancy was gone. The old
pride was gone. That bitter, volatile, cruel, vindictive spirit
was gone. Humbling himself, the king bowed, lifting up his
eyes to heaven, giving glory to God. Ah, what a scene!
Would you not have liked to have been there that day and

have witnessed the colossal, heavenly change in the life of that golden monarch?

The King Praises God

The first thing Nebuchadnezzar did was to praise the Lord. "Now I Nebuchadnezzar praise and extol and honour the King of heaven" (Dan. 4:37). In his testimony he asked the whole world to know, to listen and to rejoice with him. "Nebuchadnezzar, the king, unto all people and nations and languages that dwell in the whole earth. It is good for me that I tell you the wonders that God hath wrought toward me." The testimony of that heathen king! Should we be ashamed of what the Lord has done for us? Should this heathen king out-speak, out-testify, and out-witness us who have been saved by the cross of sacrifice, by the love, tears and grace of the Son of God? What of me? Are there no words of testimony by which I can thank Jesus for the grace and mercy that is extended to me? Dying for my sins, raised for my justification, interceding in heaven that I might finally someday make it through those golden gates and glorious streets, O Lord, are there no words that I can speak to thank Thee for that? Are there no sentences that I can say? Have I no prayers and praise of exaltation and gratitude? Lord, where are my testimonies and my expressions of thankfulness? God, touch my tongue.

"But, pastor," you say, "you do not realize. I am not gifted in speaking and in testifying." Listen, we are not asked to be philosophers, metaphysicians, theologians, and logicians. We are but to say what God has done for us and what Christ means to us. "This is what I have felt in my heart. This is what I have seen with my eyes." That is logic and rhetoric of the sublimest order. That is philosophy and theology that burns. It is touched with a coal of fire from the altar of God.

I, personally, do not know how to say it. I do not have the syllables, sentences, words, language and vocabulary to put it into meaning. But this I know. At one time I was lost, and now I am found. Once I was blind, and now I see. I have found the Lord! Oh, blessed is His name! Praises to His majesty! Oh, glory to God, I have been saved! I have given my heart to Jesus! Always and everywhere our testimonies, sweetly, quietly, beautifully, deeply and meaningfully, ought to be laid as a sacrifice of love, prayer and praise at our Savior's feet. He has changed me. He has saved me. He has taken out the beast heart and given to me a new heart. I have been cleansed in the blood of His Son, opened to His grace and guidance, fixed on Him forever. All people, nations and languages of the earth, listen to the wonders which God hath wrought toward me!

In the Market-place

In Babylon, high Babylon,
    What gear is bought and sold?
All merchandise beneath the sun
    That bartered is for gold;
Amber and oils from far beyond
    The desert and the fen,
And wines whereof our throats are fond —
    Yea! and the souls of men!

In Babylon, gray Babylon,
    What goods are sold and bought?
Vesture of linen subtly spun,
    And cups from agate wrought;
Raiment of many-colored silk
    For some fair denizen,
And ivory more white than mild —
    Yea! and the souls of men!

In Babylon, sad Babylon,
    What chattels shall invite?
A wife whenas your youth is done,
    Or leman for a night.
Before Astarte's portico
    The torches flare again;
The shadows come, the shadows go —
    Yea! and the souls of men!
                              — *George Sterling*

From *The Old Testament and the Fine Arts,* edited by Cynthia Pearl Maus, p. 639. Copyright, 1954, by Harper and Brothers.

MYSTERY BABYLON

CHAPTER 3

MYSTERY BABYLON

The king spake, and said, Is not this great Babylon,
that I have built for the house of the kingdom by the
might of my power, and for the honour of my majesty?
Daniel 4:30

In our preaching through the Book of Daniel, we read in 4:29 that Nebuchadnezzar walked in the palace of the kingdom of Babylon. "The king spake, and said, Is not this great Babylon?" He was either on top of one of those gigantic ziggurats, or on the roof of his luxurious and spacious mansion. I can see the king standing in the middle of his courtiers and with a sweep of his hand from horizon to horizon, as the great city spreads out in gold before him, he asks, "Is not this great Babylon, that I have built for the house of the kingdom by the might of my power, and for the honour of my majesty?" Babylon. As there is a God and a Satan, a Christ and an anti-christ, a kingdom of light and a kingdom of darkness, a heaven and a hell, so there is in time and space and history and Scripture a Holy City, Jerusalem, and a city of the world, Babylon. Throughout the pages of the Word of the Lord you will find that golden city of Babylon presented. We will look first at the history of this capital of Babylonia.

THE HISTORY OF BABYLON

In Genesis 10:9 we are told that Nimrod, the mighty hunter, founded a city, and he called it "Babel," the "Gate of

49

God." He built it on the plain of Shinar, an area the Assyrians called "Chaldea," (Kaldu), and the Greeks, "Babylonia."

In Genesis 11 there is another variation given to the name of the city of Babylon. Nimrod called it "Babel," the "Gate of God." But a judgment from God upon the city caused the Hebrews to find another meaning in the name. The citizens of the great plain of Shinar sought to build a tower that would pierce the sky. Not that they hoped to reach heaven by it, but they were building a great tower (a ziggurat in their language) to scan the heavens. There the Chaldean priests searched the constellations and the stars and mapped out, according to their horoscopic evaluations and prognostications, the destinies of all men and nations, seeking thereby to control all of humanity. In contempt the Lord God came down and scattered them, and He did it by a confusion of tongues. So in the Bible every time the name is mentioned in the Hebrew text, it is "Babel," a word which, the Hebrews said, came from the root "balal," "confusion." The term came to refer to a city that opposed God in its system of religion, culture and commerce.

That country then (not now for the climate has changed) was the Garden of Eden. The Scriptures describe the Tigris and Euphrates Rivers which ran through it. Those are the two rivers we can identify in the Garden of Eden. They looked upon the area as a "paradise," the Persian word for "park." The valley was formed by the alluvial deposit of those two great rivers coming out of the mountainous country of Armenia. The alluvial soil was unusually fertile and productive. It was watered by uncounted numbers of interlinking canals and waterways. The climate was soft and salubrious. It looked like a paradise, a scenic garden. It was fertile and emerald green. The whole country and land was one of prolific productiveness.

The first inhabitants of the country were Sumerians, and

they called their land Sumer. Then waves of Semitic people through the centuries poured into the area and when we come to know it in the history of the Bible, it is a Semitic land. The Assyrians, the Amorites, the Arameans, the Babylonians, and the Hebrews were Semites. From the Semitic people came Abraham, the first Hebrew.

Archaeologists, digging in the cradle of Babylon, have identified civilizations which go back eight thousand years before Christ. The land has a fantastic history. We first know the area for its great Babylonian kingdom ruled over by the famous Hammurabi. Hammurabi reigned over Babylonia for forty-three years. It was out of his kingdom that Abraham left from Ur of Chaldea, one of the cities of Babylonia, to set his face toward the Promised Land in Canaan.

As the centuries passed, there was another able king in Babylonia named Nebuchadnezzar, Nebuchadnezzar I. He was a tremendous monarch. He conquered the Elamites and then the Hittites. But he finally lost his kingdom to the Assyrians. This was in 1100 B.C. Thereafter the Assyrian empire covered the entire civilized earth. Babylonia became a subjugated province of the great empire of Assyria, with its capital on the Tigris River at Nineveh. But all through those centuries of Assyrian sovereignty, the province of Babylonia was restive and rebellious. For example, in 700 B.C. Babylonia had a king named Merodach-Baladan who is presented in Isaiah 39. He said to Hezekiah, "Let us rebel against Assyria." This Merodach-Baladan had revolted three times against Assyria and twice had crowned himself king. Hezekiah was so flattered by the interest of the king of Babylonia, that he took Merodach's emissaries on a tour of the Royal Treasury. This occasioned the rebuke of the prophet Isaiah who denounced the king of Judah because of his inordinate pride. "Hezekiah, what you have done and the relationship you have established with the heathen king of Chaldea will result in the deportation of Judea and Jerusalem as captives into that far away land of Babylon."

This Merodach-Baladan continually refused to acknowledge the sovereignty of Assyria until finally Sennacherib, one of the ablest generals of all time and the Assyrian king, came with his army and destroyed the city of Babylon utterly. He even turned the waters of the Euphrates River over the site. But in a strange providence of life his son, Esarhaddon, had it rebuilt, and his son, the great Assyrian emperor, Ashurbanipal, also followed the same policy of interest in Babylon. It was Ashurbanipal who sent down to Babylon a viceroy by the name of Nabopolassar. Nabopolassar was of Chaldean origin. He so entrenched himself in Chaldea that he was able to revolt against Assyria and proclaim himself king of Babylonia. He was a shrewd and a gifted general. He made covenants with other nations which were parts of the Assyrian empire. He took his son, Nebuchadnezzar II, and married him to Amytis, the princess of Media. Nabopolassar and the kings of the Medes and the Scythians, along with the hoards of the East, destroyed forever the Assyrian empire and plunged Nineveh so completely into obliteration that when Alexander the Great later marched his army over it, he never even realized the vast city and its great civilization lay buried beneath his feet.

In 605 B.C. Nebuchadnezzar, the son of Nabopolassar, was on his way to subjugate Egypt. He stopped by Jerusalem, besieged it and took it. But there he heard of the death of his father. So Nebuchadnezzar took Daniel and his three friends, and a few others of the royal family and hastened back to Babylon, there to consolidate his throne. He was then just twenty years of age. With his Chaldean armies, he swept over the civilized world until the whole earth belonged to Nebuchadnezzar. He never lost a battle. When the days of subjugation were over, the then known world lay under Babylonian rule, from India to Egypt, up through Mesopotamia into the land of the Armenians and the Hittites down to the Perisan Gulf from side to side.

NEBUCHADNEZZAR BUILDS THE GOLDEN CITY

When the armies no longer marched and there was no more need for warfare, Nebuchadnezzar came back to the city of Babylon to turn his attention to the building of his capital city. It had been destroyed a hundred years before by Sennacherib. So Nebuchadnezzar set himself to building the greatest, grandest, most golden city of the world. And he succeeded. There has never been before, there has never been since, and there will never ever be another city like Babylon. Nebuchadnezzar had at his disposal hundreds of thousands of slaves. If you build anything today, you may go bankrupt paying the construction costs. You may be able to build a little building on the street, twenty stories high, covering a quarter or half block, but you will find that it costs millions of dollars. But Nebuchadnezzar had no labor problems and no financial problems. He had hundreds of thousands of slaves from nations he had subjugated. He uprooted them and brought them into Babylon. There they labored to realize the dream of the great king.

Not only did Nebuchadnezzar have slave labor which cost him nothing, but he also had the treasures of the world at his command. Wherever the armies of the cruel and merciless Chaldeans went, they stripped the nations they conquered and brought back into the city the treasures of the then known world. For example, Nebuchadnezzar destroyed the temple of Solomon and brought back into Babylon all the golden altars, lampstands and utensils of the beautiful temple of Solomon. That was a peccadillo compared to the treasures which he pillaged and gathered forcefully and coercively from the ends of the earth. He had the opportunity which no man will ever have again. And he built the most beautiful city eyes have ever beheld in human history.

These things are not mythological. There were eyewitnesses who looked upon them. One was Herodotus, the first known historian. Even though Herodotus, the great Greek traveler, was there about a hundred years after Nebuchadnezzar, when the city was in its decline, yet to that Greek, Babylon was the seventh wonder of the world. Herodotus knew Athens. He knew the famous Greek cities of the Mediterranean world. But to him, there was nothing like Babylon. It was beyond imagination. Ctesias, the Greek physician, a contemporary of Herodotus, visited Babylon and surveyed it extensively. We have the records of Diodorus, and the geographer, Strabo, and the man of letters, Pliny. Besides these, many others from ancient times wrote of the glory of Babylon. And in the Scriptures you will find in both Isaiah and in Jeremiah the description of Babylon as a golden city, a woman with a golden cup in her hand (Isa. 13:19; Jer. 51:7). Now let us visit it. We are going to look at it as Herodotus did.

There it stands, surrounded by a high wall. It is built in an exact square, set toward the cardinal points of the earth. Fifteen miles this way is a wall, fifteen that way, fifteen that way, and fifteen back again. The wall is 350 feet high. It is 87 feet broad at the top, so wide that six chariots can race around it breast to breast. It is pierced by 100 gates and the gates are made of two great leaves hammered out of burnished bronze. The writers say that when the sun rose in the morning and set in the evening, those gates looked like liquid fire. Everything in Babylon was symmetrical. Twenty-five avenues, 150 feet wide, ran from east to west. Twenty-five avenues 150 feet wide, ran from north to south. In the center of the city there was an avenue which crossed over a great bridge above the Euphrates River. On that side of the avenue was a regal palace. On this side another regal palace. The Euphrates ran diagonally through the city. Between the wall of the city and the river there were guays and wharfs for the commerce of the world.

The palaces of Nebuchadnezzar were colossal. The ruins of one of Nebuchadnezzar's palaces cover now more than eleven identifiable acres. That is just one mansion. Into those palaces Nebuchadnezzar had brought the treasures of the world. They were gilded and silvered. The great banquet hall had in it the finest plastered walls. Against one of those plastered walls, the heavenly hand wrote "Mene, Mene, Tekel, Upharsin," in the days of Belshazzar, Nebuchadnezzar's profligate grandson.

Nebuchadnezzar was married by his father, Nabopolassar, to Amytis, the princess of Media. She was a mountain girl and the flat, alluvial plain of Babylon was boring to her. So the king built a mountain for her. Terraced, and covered with trees, shrubs and flowers, one could see from afar the famous hanging gardens of Babylon. When Herodotus looked upon it with his Greek compeers, they called it one of the seven wonders of the world.

The temples of Babylon also were fabulous. Into those temples Nebuchadnezzar brought the treasures of the whole earth and dedicated them to his gods. The utensils of gold and silver from Solomon's temple were there. The city was filled with temples. Some were dedicated to stars. Some were dedicated to gods such as Nebo and Ishtar and to Beltis, the spouse of Marduk. (The Hebrews spelled his name Merodach.) The temple of Merodach was composed of an outer court, a central court, and an inner court. In the inner court was the shrine to a thousand gods and goddesses. Towering against the sky was the great, rising, pyramiding ziggurat. Up and up it went, six hundred feet high. On top of that vast pile was the shrine to Marduk or Merodach. They called him "lord," in their language, "Bel," in Canaanite language, "Baal." In that shrine was a golden statue of Bel, called Bel-Merodach. It was forty-nine feet tall. Around the image all the furniture was of solid gold. One ancient historian estimated that in that one shrine alone were eight hundred talents of gold. A talent is a weight indicating all the gold that a strong man can carry. There were eight hundred talents of gold in that one shrine. No wonder the Bible calls it a golden city.

But to me, the most impressive thing about that city as I have been able to imagine it, was not the gold, not the silver, and not all the treasures of the earth that were brought into it. To me, the most magnificently impressive thing about the city would have been its color. Being on an alluvial plain, the mountains being far away, the city found little stone available for construction, so Nebuchadnezzar employed colored, enameled tile. In the heart of the city, beginning at the Ishtar gate, and running throughout the length of the city was a great procession street. It was a causeway, raised higher than the houses. On either side was built a tremendous wall with towers. The street was paved with stone, but Nebuchadnezzar lined the walls, as he did the palaces and as he did the temples, with enameled, colored tile. Those tiles depicted scenes, flora, fauna, kings, queens, and the history of the golden city.

There is a little section of Bangkok, about a half dozen blocks of it, filled with temples which are made out of porcelain — colored tile. I first saw them in 1950 and when I looked at them I thought I had never seen anything like them in my life. You can make tile any color. When you build with stone, you are limited; but when you build with man-made tile, there is no limit. When I looked at those temples in Bangkok and the color of those tiles, it was astonishing to me. Can you imagine, then, what Babylon must have looked like? Not a few blocks of it, as in Bangkok, but miles and miles of it. The most gloriously colored, most beautifully decorated city the world has ever seen was Babylon. "Is not this great Babylon, that I have built for the house of the kingdom by the might of my power, and for the honour of my majesty?" That indefatigable builder, Nebuchadnezzar, reigned over that kingdom for forty-three years. With the treasures of the earth, and with the slavery of the nations, he built that great city. It is fantastically unimaginable what that golden city looked like.

THE AWESOME JUDGMENT OF GOD UPON BABYLON

The decline and decay of Babylon is no less fantastic than its golden history. Its destruction came to be utter and complete. This happened according to the Word of the Lord. Isaiah raised up his prophetic voice and said: "And Babylon, the glory of kingdoms, the beauty of the Chaldees' excellency, shall be as when God overthrew Sodom and Gomorrah. It shall never be inhabited, neither shall it be dwelt in from generation to generation: neither shall the Arabian pitch tent there; neither shall the shepherds make their fold there. But wild beasts of the desert shall lie there; and their houses shall be full of doleful creatures; and owls shall dwell there, and satyrs shall dance there. And the wild beasts of the islands shall cry in their desolate houses, and dragons in their pleasant palaces: and her time is near to come, and her days shall not be prolonged" (Isa. 13:19-22). Jeremiah raised his voice and said, "Therefore the wild beasts of the desert with the wild beasts of the islands shall dwell there, and the owls shall dwell therein: and it shall be no more inhabited for ever; neither shall it be dwelt in from generation to generation" (Jer. 50:39). I can hardly conceive of that. Isaiah spoke his prophecy a hundred years before Nebuchadnezzar was born. When Jeremiah spoke, it was during the zenith of the glory of Nebuchadnezzar.

The city had already had a history of 7,500 years. It appeared to be impregnable. It covered an area so large the people could raise their own food inside it. They never looked for water because the Euphrates River watered the entire city. It was protected by a great moat on the outside of the wall with drawbridges at every avenue. It seemed invincible, unassailable and was located in a paradise. Yet the prophet lifted up his voice and said, "It shall be waste and barren and desert and it shall never be inhabited forever."

Austin Layard was one of the first archeologists who dug at the site of Babylon. In 1845 this is what he wrote: "Shapeless heaps of rubbish cover for many acres the face of the earth. . . . On all sides fragments of glass, marble, pottery, and inscribed brick are mingled with that peculiar nitrous and blanched soil which, bred from the remains of ancient habitations, checks or destroys vegetation, and renders the site of Babylon a naked and hideous waste. Owls start from the scanty thickets and the foul jackel skulks through the furrows." For centuries the drifting sands of the desert have buried it out of sight. The winding sheet of silence broods over it. The judgment of Almighty God! Whether a nation lives or not, whether a civilization endures or not, whether a city continues or not, is an imponderable in the hands of Almighty God. There has never been a city so apparently indestructible as Babylon. Even when Alexander the Great intended to make Babylon the center of his empire and to build again its mighty fortresses. But Alexander was cut down, as you know — murdered in Babylon.

Mystery Babylon in Prophecy

In prophetic Scripture what does God say about Babylon? God calls it "Mystery, Babylon the great, the mother of harlots and abominations of the earth." The seventeenth chapter of the Revelation begins with these words, "Come hither; I will shew unto thee the judgment of the great whore that sitteth upon many waters" (Rev. 17:5). What does that mean? She represents the religious system that is unfaithful to God. These who serve in that system purport to be servants of God, but they are spiritual whores, harlots and prostitutes. That is what God says.

Could it be actually true that there are purported servants of God who are unfaithful to Him? Look at this and lament. A popular magazine hired pollsters to survey all the seminaries of America. They were to find out what kind of preachers we are to have in the next generation. Seventy-one percent of the preachers surveyed did not believe in an after-life. They believe that when you die, you die like a dog. Sixty percent do not believe in the Virgin Birth, nor do they believe in the resurrection from the dead. Ninety-eight percent do not believe we will ever see Jesus again. And a large percent do not believe at all in a personal God. They believe in an *it*, in a motion, in some kind of an indescribable, ephemeral principle which they speak of in metaphysical terms. They do not believe in a personal God although they are supposed to represent Him. They are prostitutes, harlots, standing in the name of Christ and in the name of God and in the churches of the Lord but denying the faith. "Come, I'll show you the judgment of God upon the great whore."

The woman sits upon a scarlet-colored beast, having the names of blasphemy and her name is "Mother of Harlots, The Great Babylon." Let us look at these Greek words in order that we can see the full import of her description. She is full of "sorcerers and sorceresses." What were these "sorcerers"? The original language will tell us. The Greek word "pharmakon" is literally, "drug." It is the Greek word for black magic, taking trips, using some kind of chemical to have feelings of religion. The Greek word used to describe the one who leads in that chemical experience is "phar-makos," "magician," translated here, "sorcerer." The Greek word "pharmakeia" is translated "sorcery," "magic." That is where our English word "pharmacist" comes from, refer-ring to one who deals in drugs. Where did all this present day drug culture come from? It originated in Babylon. It is not new, this addiction that purposes to use drugs to get people up tight with ethereal trips.

The curse of the harlot Babylon with her false experience of religion by drugs is increasingly becoming the curse of America. "Mystery Babylon" is repeated today in "Mystery New York," "Mystery San Francisco," "Mystery Dallas," and "Mystery Cities of America and of the World." Recently I attended a White House Conference on drugs. I was over-whelmed by the magnitude of the problem, a problem which is basically religious-spiritual, one that follows the false sys-tems of Babylon and, as a governmental official stated, "the final answer to which is beyond the reach of government." It costs the American taxpayer eight billion dollars a year to face that problem.

I quote from the President. He said he was surprised that addiction starts at such an early age, as young as twelve years of age. We cannot approach the problem with anger, he said, but with sorrow. We can be angry at the pusher, at the junkie, but not at the addict. We must seek rehabilita-tion rather than punishment. Why does a young person give up on the democratic system to turn to something he thinks leads to a way out, but it does not? That young person has a spiritual need, the President said. He has a spiritual need that must be filled. He told us that if there is an answer, you gentlemen have it. That young person must have something to believe in, something to which he can turn. The worst thing that can happen to a young person is to have no faith and no belief in anything. The heart of the problem is a spiritual vacuum. That is the judgment of the President of the United States. The Babylonian system leads to ultimate destruction.

Drug addiction is spelled D-E-A-T-H. I hold in my hand a UPI story out of the daily newspaper. It is datelined Tacoma, Washington. I read from the UPI news story:

> A railroad employee found the well-dressed body of a young man in a corner of an empty boxcar behind the Union Pacific depot. In the jacket pocket were empty pill boxes and a billfold identifying the youth as (then it goes on and tells about the boy). When the body was moved a suicide note was found. It said, "Dear Dad, Dope ruined my life and took away my happiness forever. I thought I was experiencing life. I found it was death. I hope to God people taking dope find what I found in it sooner than I did. Good-by, Dad, your son, Love, Ricky."

You spell dope addiction D-E-A-T-H.

I went to Haight-Ashbury. I was out there two or three times, just looking at it. The Haight-Ashbury District in San Francisco originally captured the attention of the world because of the idealistic flower children who converged there. It looked as if there were appearing on the horizon of American life a new, glorious phenomenon. Young people would travel all over the country to see it. They had heard vaguely about the drug overtone involved but had no introduction to it. Into what did Haight-Ashbury develop? A knowledgeable writer spent many weeks with the youngsters on the streets, on the pads and in their rooms. Now I am going to quote from him.

"This is the end of the flower children, the hippie movement. . . . They would share their food, most of which had been panhandled on the streets. They would talk readily about free love but very little about the alarming rise of venereal disease brought on by such practices. They even wore buttons saying 'Syphilis can be fun.' Gradually the idealism of the streets gave way to con-artists, thugs, exploiters and hard-core pushers and junkies who made the whole community their victim. Peace and love are gone from the streets of the district today. All that remains is crime and violence and death." Drug addition is spelled D-E-A-T-H.

But not only did harlot Babylon deal in drug magic, she also was the mother of the astrologers and of those who deceive the gullible public with horoscopy. In the beginning of Babel, the people raised a great tower to obtain a clearer view of the heavens. The Chaldean priests were gazing at the stars as they stood on those ziggurats or temples. "Hora" in Greek means "hour." "Skopos" means "watcher." The two words together make our English word "horoscope." The priests inquired into the exact hour of your birth and set your "horoscope." In gazing at the stars the astrologers figured to tell you the fixed destiny of your life, whether you were king, queen, or slave. That is where that word "kismet" came from, "fate." The Babylonian astrologers taught the world that there is no personal God to whom we can make appeal and by whom a man can hope to change his life. Rather his life is governed by the stars, by a destiny which was set when he was born. All this fake instruction came from Chaldea and has continued through the centuries to this present age. That is a facet of religious Babylon and it is a practice followed by millions who today read the horoscopic predictions in our city newspapers.

The eighteenth chapter of Revelation speaks of commercial Babylon. The great and mighty city was the pride of the merchants of the earth. They sold precious stones, silver and gold, pearls, linen and purple silk, ivory, brass, frankincense, oil, wheat, sheep, horses, chariots, slaves, and a thousand other things. But Revelation 18:13 concludes the list with trafficking in the "souls of men." This was commercial Babylon in ancient days. It is commercial Babylon today. What would the world of entertainment care if they destroyed thousands and thousands of lives "trafficking in the souls of men"? Babylon has a commercial system which is anti-God. What does China or Russia care if two-thirds of the earth are starved and dead as long as the few who remain are Marxists? "Trafficking in the souls of men."

Babylon represents the system which God shall someday judge as He did Sodom and Gomorrah. In Revelation 14:8 an angel cries, "Babylon is fallen, is fallen, that great city." Now, look at that same identical phrase used by a mighty angel in 18:2, "Babylon the great is fallen, is fallen." It would have been enough to say once, "Babylon is fallen." But in both passages the angel says it twice. What does it mean? The first "fallen" refers to the system of spiritual unfaithfulness that dishonors our Lord. That is finally judged and "fallen." The second "fallen" refers to the great commercial and cultural life of the people in the world which is anti-God, a system that leaves God out of life, out of culture, out of literature, out of commerce, and out of the dreams, hopes and visions of the future. Political leaders, national leaders and state leaders who turn from the will of God face an inevitable judgment. Babylon as a commercial system ends in tragic destruction.

The Book says that when we link our lives with that kingdom of darkness, we purchase for our souls eternal damnation. When the system goes down, we go down with it. When we link our lives with these movements represented by golden Babylon, the end thereof is desolation, disaster, and death. Fire, fury, and certain loss, ruin, and damnation will fall upon us. The whole tragedy is summed up in that awesome word "hell," cast down to hell. Oh, the judgments of Almighty God!

That is why the Lord came. That is why He became incarnate. He left His throne in glory and came down here among men to deliver us from so awesome a judgment. To those who turn in living faith to that living Lord, God has promised an abundant life. Every day is a better day with the Lord. If you are a business man and Christ is your partner, it is a better day where you work. If you are in the world of arts and culture, and Christ is your inspiration, every creation is a better picture, a better song. And if you serve in the world of religion, my world, you who will honor Christ, Christ will honor. When we link our lives with God, God links His life with us. It is great now; it is greater tomorrow; and it is greatest in that glorious new world the Lord has prepared for those who love Him. That is our invitation today. Give your heart to the Lord. Link your life to the life of God. Open your heart to the blessed Jesus. Come out of the kingdom of Babylon into the kingdom of Christ Jesus. In Babylon we shall surely fall and die. But in Jesus we shall be lifted up to live forever. Give your life to Him.

BELSHAZZAR

Midnight came slowly sweeping on;
In silent rest lay Babylon.

But in the royal castle high
Red torches gleam and courtiers cry.

Belshazzar there in kingly hall
Is holding kingly festival.

The vassals sat in glittering line,
And emptied the goblets with glowing wine.

The goblets rattle, the choruses swell,
And it pleased the stiff-necked monarch well.

In the monarch's cheeks a wild fire flowed,
And the wine awoke his daring mood.

And, onward still by his madness spurred,
He blasphemes the Lord with a sinful word;

And he brazenly boasts, blaspheming wild,
While the servile courtiers cheered and smiled.

Quick the king spoke, while his proud glance burned,
Quickly the servant went and returned.

He bore on his head the vessels of gold,
Of Jehovah's temple the plunder bold.

With daring hand, in his frenzy grim,
The king seized a beaker and filled to the brim,

And drained to the dregs the sacred cup,
And foaming he cried, as he drank it up,

"Jehovah, eternal scorn I own
To thee, I am monarch of Babylon."

Scarce had the terrible blasphemy rolled
From his lips, ere the monarch at heart was cold.

The yelling laughter was hushed, and all
Was still as death in the royal hall.

And see! and see! on the white wall high
The form of a hand went slowly by,

And wrote — and wrote, on the broad wall white,
Letters of fire, and vanished in night.

Pale as death, with a steady stare,
And with trembling knees, the king sat there;

The horde of slaves sat huddering chill;
No word they spoke, but were deathlike still.

The Magicians came, but of them all,
None could read the flame-script on the wall.

But that same night, in all his pride,
By the hands of his servants Belshazzar died.

— *Heinrich Heine*

From *The Old Testament and the Fine Arts* edited by Cynthia Pearl Maus, pp. 711, 712. Copyright, 1954, by Harper & Brothers.

DRUNK KINGS

CHAPTER 4

DRUNK KINGS

Belshazzar the king made a great feast to a thousand of his lords, and drank wine before the thousand.

Belshazzar, whiles he tasted the wine, commanded to bring the golden and silver vessels which his father Nebuchadnezzar had taken out of the temple which was in Jerusalem; that the king, and his princes, his wives, and his concubines, might drink therein.

Then they brought the golden vessels that were taken out of the temple of the house of God which was at Jerusalem; and the king, and his princes, his wives, and his concubines, drank in them.

They drank wine, and praised the gods of gold, and of silver, of brass, of iron, of wood, and of stone.

Daniel 5:1-4

In our preaching through the book of Daniel we have come to Chapter 5, and the message is an exposition of the first four verses.

DAYS OF DECADENCE

This is the first scene in a chapter of human history that rushes by like a torrent. The king and his court hold an orgy. The scene is full of defamation, desecration, blasphemy, judgment, and the awesome intervention of God. It ends in the loss of the first golden kingdom of the Gentiles. It all happened within a few hours of the desolation of the

Babylonian empire. The head of gold has turned to mud, filth, and excess. In the story we have a glimpse of the last days of decadence of any civilization. All civilizations seem to follow the same pattern. Immorality and drunkenness increase. Finally, evil grows to such vast proportions that the ripened fruit rots and hell itself opens and yawns. "The wicked shall be turned into hell, and all the nations that forget God" (Ps. 9:17). We see here in Daniel the atmosphere of the days of Noah and the days of Sodom and Gomorrah.

"Belshazzar, the king, made a great feast." There is no harm in making a great feast, but that is where the devil begins. He always begins where there is no harm. Feasts by the thousands were held in ancient Babylon, and still today many kings or rulers make great feasts. But beware. This Satan is a subtle beast, the most subtle of the beasts which God created. His innocent suggestions are prompted by ulterior motives.

For example, Satan said to the Lord Jesus: "You are hungry. For forty days and nights You have fasted, so turn these stones into bread." How innocent the suggestion, but Satan was and is the deceiver and the assassin of mankind. What he attempted to achieve was the undoing of the incarnation. Jesus came down to be a man, to live like a man, to be incarnate in human flesh. And men do not turn stones into bread. We are to work and to earn our bread. Satan always begins with an innocent suggestion — "There is no harm in it."

The relationship between a boy and a girl is something which God made. But Satan begins there and carries them to destruction. To smoke a reefer, a joint, a marijuana cigarette is such a slight sin in his book of enticements. "There is no harm in it." The devil begins there, but the end in addiction is so often tragic.

You are the treasurer of the store, or of the bank. Satan

whispers: "What is it to borrow a little money? You are going to pay it back." Maybe you are the treasurer of the church. You are going to *borrow* a little money. You will pay it back. There is no harm in it. Satan always begins there with innocent suggestions.

TEMPESTUOUS TIMES

There is nothing wrong in a feast, but you will see that this feast was different. The king invited a thousand of his lords. And everyone of them had his retinue, his guard, his favorite females, his dancers, musicians, jugglers, and entertainers. By the time they were congregated, there were at least ten thousand in that vast banquet hall in ancient Babylon. But the time of the feast, the setting of it, was unbelievable, unthinkable, and unimaginable. Outside those walls his father, Nabonidus, was fighting for his throne, for his kingdom, and for his life. He was warring against the invading hordes of the Medes and Persians under King Cyrus. And Nabonidus, the Babylonian king, had been defeated. He was shut up a refugee in Borsippa. All around that city of Babylon on every side, as you stood on top of the walls, as far as you could see in every direction, were the camps of the Medes and Persians. At a time when his father was fighting and warring for the life of the empire, this profligate and voluptuous son called for an orgy of his lords and his concubines. They reveled and they drank to the unseemly, unnamable gods of dirt, filth, corruption, sin and excess. It is hard to believe. And yet, as I read that story, I think how common and how ordinary it is. Every day there are noble fathers and noble mothers whose unworthy sons betray them and bring their heads down to grief and despair.

At a luncheon I attended in the White House recently, one of the heads of state read a letter. It was one of the most heartbreaking communications I have ever heard. It was written by a famous professor in a university, a world famed university in New England. In that letter he said, "We brought up our boy in the Lord, to honor his country and to revere his home and parents." The letter continued: "Our son is a dropout. He interprets freedom as freedom for love and promiscuity. He interprets democracy as an open opportunity to defame our institutions and to seek for the overthrow of our country. And he despises his father and his mother. He lives in filth and on drugs." This is a description of bestial Belshazzar.

Nabonidus, by the way, was one of the most cultured kings who ever lived. He was an antiquarian and an archaeologist. He was not much of a soldier but he was a noble man in all of his interests. While Nabonidus was outside the city fortress, fighting for his life, Belshazzar, his profligate and corrupted son, called together this orgy. As they assembled, there he stood in the midst of them, behind his impregnable, unassailable and invincible walls. He did not realize that what generations of men have erected and built, and what seems to be unassailable and invincible, can be destroyed by debauchery in an hour.

In preparing for this message, I read one author who said the Medes and Persians had been besieging Babylon two and one half years when this incident happened. Other historians say the siege had been going on for many months. These same authors declare that after the months, possibly after the years, of besieging the city, the Medes and the Persians were in the process of withdrawing. It seemed to be the only impregnable bastion they had ever faced. Cyrus, the king, had conquered the entire east. Only one jewel lay unclaimed, and that was the city of Babylon. Desperately they had tried to take it. They had assaulted and besieged it on every side, and failing, had finally begun to withdraw. It was unassailable. It was not open to the aggressive power of men. It was that very time, when the enemy could not reach the walls or scale the towers, that this profligate son called together his licentious revelry.

It was in that same place, in that same city, and in that same palace (two hundred years later), that Alexander the Great (undefeated by the armies of the world) fell and lost his life in a drunken debauchery. It was in this same place, in one hour, in one night, in the same kind of alcoholic orgy that Belshazzar met his judgment.

It is an astonishing thing to me how much there is in the Bible about strong drink. God speaks to the rulers of the people, to the kings of commerce, to the kings of industry, to the kings of finance, and to the kings of states, nations, and cities, about wine. Listen to this: "The words of king Lemuel, the prophecy that his mother taught him. What, my son? and what, the son of my womb? and what, the son of my vows? It is not for kings, O Lemuel, it is not for kings to drink wine; nor for princes strong drink: lest they drink, and forget the law, and pervert the judgment of any of the afflicted" (Prov. 31:1, 2, 4, 5). And Solomon said: "Who hath woe? who hath sorrow? who hath contentions? who hath babbling? who hath wounds without cause? who hath redness of eyes? They that tarry long at the wine; they that go to seek mixed wine. Look not thou upon the wine when it is red, when it giveth his colour in the cup, when it moveth itself aright. At the last it biteth like a serpent, and stingeth like an adder" (Prov. 23:29-32). Look again at Solomon as he writes, "Wine is a mocker, strong drink is raging: and whosoever is deceived thereby is not wise" (Prov. 20:1).

A bride was urged by her father to drink a toast of wine to her husband and to her home. She refused, but the father blatantly pushed her on. The young bride finally lifted up the glass of wine and said, "Its color and its sparkle mock me for therein I see a divorced husband, a broken-hearted wife, a grieving mother, and a darkened, saddened home — our home." "Ah," you say, "such ministerial stupidity!" Listen, if you combine all of the addicts in the world — those who take hallucinogenics, those who take narcotics, those who take barbiturates, and those who take amphetamines — the total of them all is not a drop in the bucket compared to the uncounted millions whose lives now are destroyed and are being destroyed by that glass of liquor. The preacher is a fool, you say. Then God is a fool, for I just read out of the Word of the Lord.

While we are speaking of the curse of alcohol, let us drive home the naked truth of our modern, compromised American attitude toward the legalized liquor traffic.

The Hypocritical Attitude of Modern American Babylons Toward Alcohol (Liquid Pot)

The message of American advertising is, "Cure your pains by chemicals." Adults set up powerful examples. There is the "necessary" cigarette. Many cannot last through an evening without nicotine. There is the liquor before dinner. There are the diet pills, the sleeping pills, the tranquilizing pills. When these same parents see their teenagers use drugs, they call them fiends and criminals and degenerates. The young people merely are following in their parents' and society's footsteps. If there ever lived a hypocritical culture and a hypocritical generation, it is the present culture and the present generation of American citizens.

Marijuana is no more intoxicating and no more addictive and no more fraught with overtones of tragedy than alcohol. Let us look at this attitude toward liquor, which is liquid pot. Never, never is it proposed to attack liquor or to oppose it as they do other drugs. We are getting to the place where we are willing to face nicotine and the deadly effects of tobacco. We are beginning to say to the advertising media: "You can't bring that stuff into our living room and present it there before our children. It has death in the package. There is emphysema and lung cancer." We are facing up to the truth of tobacco. But there are no proposals to face and to outlaw liquor and alcohol. Rather, the trend of our society is in the other direction.

We are talking about marijuana and alcohol, both of them drugs. One of them is liquid. The other is dry. Now look at this quote. I read from Dr. Donald B. Lourie, in his book entitled *Drug Scene*. Now listen to him. "The proponents for the legalization of marijuana point out that alcohol is a dangerous drug which is perfectly legal in our society." That is right, isn't it? The proponents for the legalization of marijuana point out that alcohol, a dangerous drug, is perfectly legal in our society. They say that marijuana is no more dangerous than alcohol. And that is right. There is not a doctor in the land who will stand up and deny that. The proponents for the legalization of marijuana say that marijuana is no more dangerous than alcohol.

Now, it seems to me that we ought to stand up and say that as we oppose marijuana we should also oppose alcohol. But the lobbyists don't ever say it. What do they say? Admitting that alcohol is a dangerous drug, they simply ask the question whether we are to add to our alcohol burden another intoxicant. In the United States there is currently a death from automobile accidents due to alcohol every eleven minutes and an injury every eighteen seconds. They simply ask whether we shall add another intoxicant, such as marijuana, and increase the number of inebriated drivers and pedestrians and attain a death rate of one every five minutes and an injury every eight seconds? Never is it proposed that we opppose all of these drugs that have devastating effects upon the mind. Never are we to oppose liquor. Liquor is a sacred cow. We dare not speak of it. We dare not touch it. But the proposal is made that we fight marijuana to the death because we already have one intoxicant drug that is decimating our people, slaughtering them on the highways, breaking up our homes and families. We already have one of them. But we do nothing about that one. It is merely that American society and American national life cannot stand another one. Therefore, we oppose the entrance of marijuana. That is the reasoning of the educational and political and economic leadership of present-day America. What cowardice!

PROFANING THE SACRED TEMPLE VESSELS

Nabonidus the father was out battling for his life. And his profligate son, Belshazzar, was inside the walls drinking in an orgy with his concubines. Tankards of wine disappeared like rivers in a forest. While he was drinking to the gods of gold, silver, iron, dust, rust, filth, and corruption, he had an inspiration. You always have inspirations when you are drunk. So with Belshazzar. While the wine boiled in his veins and inflamed his mind, he had an inspiration. His grandfather, Nebuchadnezzar, had plundered and pillaged the holy Temple in Jerusalem, and had taken out of the "holy city" the beautiful articles of furniture and vessels of gold and silver. Drunk and inspired by the devil the inebriated king said: "Send for those sacred vessels. This wine deserves the finest goblets." What is sin if you do not refine it? Nebuchadnezzar had taken the beautiful vessels from Solomon's temple and had further perpetrated his wickedness by destroying the Holy City and plundering the Holy Temple. What is sin if it is not innovative and brought up to date? Belshazzar said: "My grandfather plundered the temple and took the vessels. I shall go even further in brazen effrontery to God. I shall defile them and desecrate them. I shall blaspheme the name of the God to whom they were dedicated. I shall get drunk with them."

Now, those vessels had remained holy and sacred in Babylon for seventy years. They were trophies of war and were placed in a sacred shrine. I am not exaggerating when I say to you: I can easily see every Jewish family in Babylonia taking their little boys and girls to that shrine. The father and the mother would stand there and say: "Son, you see that seven-branched golden lampstand? It burned in the holy Temple of Jehovah God in the holy city. And daughter, do you see that golden altar? On it our high priest burned incense, and our prayers went up to the name of the Holy and only God in Jerusalem. Children, do you see these goblets and these plates? On those sacred plates the shewbread was placed once every sabbath day." To the Jews, those were sacred symbols of the one true and living God.

And Belshazzar took those sacred vessels, poured wine into them, and parceled them out to his paramours, his mistresses, his concubines. His thousand lords did the same. Do you notice how the Scripture describes it here? "They drank wine and praised the gods." What gods? The passage contains this long, grim list: "gods of gold, and of silver, and of brass, and of wood, and of stone." I would not have the courage to describe the way in which they worshiped those gods of the Canaanites and of the Babylonians for it was unthinkably corrupt and vile. Engraved on artifacts recovered from that era of history are pornographic pictures and symbols of the grossest immorality. Compared to what these gods represented, and the way in which they were worshiped, present-day immorality is a child's game. They took those sacred vessels and goblets, and those plates on which the sacred shewbread once had been placed, and they blasphemed the name of Almighty God in drunkenness and public promiscuity.

The Final Word Lies With God Almighty

But there is another verse, another paragraph, another chapter to this unbelievable account. The Lord God looked down from heaven and heard the blasphemy. The title of my next chapter will be, "The Handwriting on the Wall." God always has the final word. Wherever you find sin, wherever you find national decay, you do not need a prophet to point out the handwriting on the wall. The deeper the sin, the closer the judgment. In Belshazzar we see sin and judgment side by side, back to back.

The desecration and the defamation of sacred and holy things is not peculiar to ancient Babylon. We still have it today. The Lord's Day — is it not a sacred day? Does it not belong to God? Is it not described in the Word of God itself as the Lord's own day? And yet, modern America and modern Christian people are increasingly making it not a holy day but a holiday. It is a day to forget God instead of a day to remember Him. A hundred other holy things could I name; the Lord's Day is just one of them. So many things are sacred and holy and belong to God, yet we desecrate, defame, and defile them.

A man's heart — does not the Holy Word say it is a temple of the Holy Spirit? Does not the Spirit of the Lord belong in the human heart? "What? know ye not that your body is the temple of the Holy Ghost which is in you, which ye have of God, and ye are not your own? For ye are bought with a price: therefore glorify God in your body, and in your spirit, which are God's" (I Cor. 6:19, 20). Your body is the temple of God. But who reigns on the throne of your heart? Who is there? Who sits and drives and decides and dreams and judges and directs your life? Who is on the throne, the sacred throne of your heart? Is it avarice? Lust? Greed? Pride? Self-will? Is it a thousand other gods who ought not to be there? Who ought to be enthroned in your heart? Should it not be God before whom we bow in love and admiration? Should it not be the Lord Christ who is honored in our hearts?

Lord, who is on the throne in our lives? Who reigns over

our souls? Lord, every vision we have, every dream to which we aspire, every ambition, every outreach of our lives, everything, Lord, ought to be as unto Thee. Is it? Who is enthroned in that sacred place which belongs to God alone? That is what the apostle means when he says, "I die daily" (I Cor. 15:31b). Dead to self, dead to every personal dream and ambition, and alive to Christ! Resurrected in Him!

Oh, Master, how do You do it? In our own selves we cannot. It lies in the prerogative of God. The Lord must help us. That is why we need God. We cannot do it alone. We cannot make it by ourselves. We have not the strength. It must be in God. And that is our appeal to your heart today. Let God deliver you from the muck and mire of this sinful Babylon in which we live. Enthrone Jesus in your heart. Make Him the center of your life. Instead of letting Babylon defile you, let Christ deliver you. Instead of being condemned by your own sinfulness, be cleansed by the blood of Jesus. He died to save you from this present evil world. And He will save you if you will come to Him. Do it now. Do it today.

VISION OF BELSHAZZAR

The King was on his throne, the Satraps throng'd the
    hall:
A thousand bright lamps shone o'er that high festival.
A thousand cups of gold, in Judah deem's divine —
Jehovah's vessels, hold the godless heathen's wine.

In that same hour and hall, the fingers of a hand
Came forth against the wall, and wrote as if on sand:
The fingers of a man — a solitary hand,
Along the letters ran, and traced them like a wand.

The monarch saw, and shook, and bade no more rejoice;
All bloodless wax'd his look, and tremulous his voice.
"Let the men of lore appear, the wisest of the earth,
And expound the words of fear, which mar our royal
    mirth."

Chaldea's seers are good, but here they have no skill;
And the unknown letters stood untold and awful still.
And Babel's men of age are wise and deep in lore;
But now they were not sage, they saw — but knew no
more.

A captive in the land, a stranger and a youth,
He heard the king's command, he saw that writing's
truth.
The lamps around were bright, the prophecy in view;
He read it on that night — the morrow proved it true.

"Belshazzar's grave is made, his kingdom pass'd away,
He, in the balance weighed, is light and worthless clay;
The shroud his robe of state, his canopy the stone.
The Mede is at his gate! The Persian on his throne!"

— *Lord Byron*

From *The Complete Poetical Works of Byron*, p. 220. Cambridge
Edition. Copyright, 1905, by Houghton Mifflin Company, Boston.

THE HANDWRITING ON THE WALL

CHAPTER 5

THE HANDWRITING ON THE WALL

In the same hour came forth fingers of a man's hand, and wrote over against the candlestick upon the plaster of the wall of the king's palace: and the king saw the part of the hand that wrote.

Then the king's countenance was changed, and his thoughts troubled him, so that the joints of his loins were loosed, and his knees smote one against another.

The king cried aloud to bring in the astrologers, the Chaldeans, and the soothsayers. And the king spake, and said to the wise men of Babylon, Whosoever shall read this writing, and shew me the interpretation thereof, shall be clothed with scarlet, and have a chain of gold about his neck, and shall be the third ruler in the kingdom.

Then came in all the king's wise men: but they could not read the writing, nor make known to the king the interpretation thereof.

Then was king Belshazzar greatly troubled, and his countenance was changed in him, and his lords were astonied.

Daniel 5:5-9

THE DISSOLUTE, PROFLIGATE PRINCE

The background of this orgiastic feast given by Belshazzar was presented in the previous chapter. Nabonidus, the king of Babylonia and the father of Belshazzar, was fighting for his life, for his throne, and for his kingdom against Cyrus and the Medes and the Persians. Cyrus already had destroyed the army of Nabonidus and the king, himself, was shut up in the city of Borsippa. The profligate and unworthy son of Nabonidus, Belshazzar, was co-regent with his father and reigned in the capital city of Babylon. But while his father was warring for his life, battling for the throne and the kingdom, Belshazzar was in an orgy with his concubines, his female dancers, and his gluttonous lords in the great banquet hall of Nebuchadnezzar's palace. He spreads this feast in contempt for the enemy on the outside. Cyrus and his great Medo-Persian army had been besieging the city of Babylon for months, possibly for two and a half years. But the walls were great, 350 feet high and 87 feet across. They were surrounded by a deep, broad moat, fed by the waters of the Euphrates River. The city was so large it could grow its own produce. It had water in abundance. The Euphrates flowed through its center. It was impregnable and invincible. No military device at that time could breach those walls and no army could storm those gates. In contempt, Belshazzar, within the safety of the city that could be besieged forever and never fall, threw this orgiastic festival, this unspeakable party.

But what the drunken king did not know is that the strength of a kingdom, the strength of a city, and the strength of a nation, is never on the outside, but on the inside. He did not know that an empire won by war must be consolidated by justice and righteousness. On the inside of that city of Babylon were all of those polyglot races whom Nebuchadnezzar had uprooted from their homes. He had pillaged and plundered their land and had resettled them in Babylonia and in Babylon. Among those restless races no one of those enslaved, captive nations whose homeland had been destroyed, was more restive than the Jews. They refused amalgamation with the heathen people, and they worshiped a strange God they called Jehovah, the Lord. It was in contempt for them that the inebriated king thought to bring for drunken use the sacred vessels that Nebuchadnezzar took out of the temple of Solomon in the holy city, Jerusalem. Those vessels had been sacredly kept in Babylon for seventy years. "I will send for them and we will drink out of those goblets of gold and silver," said Belshazzar. "We will defame the God of the Jews, and we will debauch His name. We will show these Jews, these people of Judah and Israel; we will show them our scornful distaste and our supercilious contempt for their faith and religion." So Belshazzar called for the holy vessels to be taken out of the shrine in which they had been kept for seventy years. At his immoral party in which they were feasting, dancing, and drinking, he employed the holy vessels to praise the gods of gold, silver, iron, stone and wood. They made the feast an effrontery to the great God of heaven. It seems that men who are weak often are superficially brought to strength by arrogance and effrontery. But at the same time they create an awesome repercussion in the souls of them whom they defame. This is especially so when the defamation touches the most sensitive part of human life, religion and faith in God.

THE HANDWRITING ON THE WALL

It was in the midst of Belshazzar's orgiastic feast that there appeared over against the lampstand, the great candelabra which shone against the white plastered wall, the fingers of a man's hand, incising words in the very stone itself. Belshazzar, the king, having made the sumptuous feast for a thousand of his lords, was on a raised platform. There, before the thousand lords, their concubines, their retinues, and their guards (there must have been at least ten thousand present), he boldly displayed his impiety and his sacrilege. They were invited to witness his effrontery and his blasphemous ostentation. There, on an elevated dais, he brazenly displayed this unspeakable insult to God in heaven.

But in the midst of it, while he was drinking and praising the heathen gods in profane ways, suddenly the cup dropped from his hand. His eyes were fixed in stark terror on the wall. The joints of his loins were loosed and his knees smote one another as his gaze was frozen on the wall. I can see the eyes of all of that vast multitude follow the eyes of the king. They, too, see that hand, incising those characters in the stone. The vast hall suddenly became as silent as death. I can see all of their eyes focus back on the king for interpretation, for courage. But instead of finding a monarch of great strength, they behold a miserably weak coward, literally paralyzed in fear. What is the matter with him? Why, a moment before, his face was flushed with wine and effrontery. But now he is so pale, he is blanched white. He has to hold to the table just to keep himself upright. What has happened to him? Some say he fell into delirium tremors. Some say he saw hieroglyphics cut into the wall on some of those bricks and his guilty conscience brought the terror. Not so. For after the hand had slowly, deliberately cut the characters into the wall, the words remained for all to behold.

> In the night as they revelled
> In a lordly palace hall,
> They were filled with consternation
> At the hand upon the wall.

The whole festive throng was thrown into a silent limbo of dread and foreboding. There were enemies on the outside, knocking at the gate of the city, but the enemies on the inside of their souls were the fiercest of all.

CONDEMNED BY CONSCIENCE AND INWARD JUDGMENT

We interpret things according to our conscience, according to the inside of our souls. That is a most amazing truth of human reaction, but it is true of all of us. It is God's approach to inevitable, inexorable judgment.

Would you not have thought that when the king led that feast of blasphemy the Lord would have struck him dead on the spot? But the Lord did nothing of the kind. The feast went right on, the drinking went right on, and the blasphemy went right on. But then, at its climax, there came in a specter, a ghost of a man's hand. You could cast out thieves and robbers and trespassers, or an uninvited guest, but how do you cast out a ghost? You can drink and drown the thoughts of God and shut Him out of your life, but how do you shut out that ghost, that conscience? How do you do it? Why did not the king interpret that writing as a marvelous omen and a glorious sign of triumph in his hour of need? He was besieged and his kingdom was on the verge of abysmal destruction. Why did he not interpret the writing as something from God, something of strength and courage and victory?

Elijah was down on his knees praying when he saw in the sky a cloud the size of a man's hand. Elijah then arose and announced victory. Why did not Belshazzar interpret that hand and that writing as a sign of victory?

The reason is in all of us and it is obvious. We interpret everything which happens in our lives according to our consciences. "Conscience doth make cowards of us all." The man in sin is afraid of anything unknown. He is terrorized by even the soft sound of a footstep outside his door. I once read of a criminal who turned himself over to the sheriff saying: "All these years I have been prostrate with fear at every knock at the door and every step on the sidewalk. I can bear the guilt no longer." Conscience is the ghost that writes upon the wall.

In the Garden of Eden, we do not know how long, how many days, how many years, God came and visited the man and the woman whom He had made. How glorious and precious for God to come down to visit the man and his wife! It was a sweet fellowship, a precious communion between the man and the Lord. But one day the couple heard the voice of the Lord God walking in the garden, in the cool of the day. They were terrified. They hid themselves from His face. Why, what had happened? They had fallen into sin and had interpreted the sound of the voice of God in the light of that ghost of conscience which you cannot shut out.

Herod Antipas, the king of Galilee, heard of the works of Jesus of Nazareth. Would you not have thought that he would have rejoiced? He was the king, and in his kingdom was a miracle worker. But when Herod heard of the work of Jesus of Nazareth, he was afraid. He was alarmed. He was seized with terror. Why? Herod, what have you done? This is what he had done. He had beheaded John the Baptist, and when he heard of the works of Christ, Herod said, "This is none other than John the Baptist raised from the dead." He interpreted the power of the Nazarene in the light of his conscience. Now, Herod Antipas by sympathy was a Sadducee. He belonged in spirit to the ruling class of Palestine, namely, the Sadducees. They did not believe in the resurrection of the dead; neither did he. But listen! Our theology is nothing in front of the handwriting on the wall. Our superficial, cheap metaphysics seems to crumble as events suddenly begin to be interpreted by our consciences. Herod Antipas, not believing in the resurrection, was still terrified. He thought Jesus was John the Baptist, raised from the dead.

Look at Felix, Roman procurator of Judea. Would you not have thought that when Paul the incomparable apostle stood before Felix and preached to him the unsearchable riches of grace in Christ Jesus that Felix would have rejoiced? But the Book says that Felix trembled. The message of truth made him afraid.

And Belshazzar. Why, his knees knocked together. When he saw those words incised on the stone wall, it terrified him. He called for the Magi. There was no ability to find an answer to this. Then the queen mother, either by reason of the words (or the noise) in the banquet hall, or else because someone told her of the terror and consternation of the king, left her apartment and appeared in the judgment hall of the great banquet room. In a world of polygamy a wife is nothing. She is just one out of a whole harem. But the queen mother (as you will read in I Kings) had a place of dignity and influence. This queen mother almost surely was Nitoricus, the daughter of Nebuchadnezzar.

THE KING CALLS FOR GOD'S MAN

The queen remembered when a great prophet of God guided her father through his maniacal madness, and brought him to the knowledge of the most High. So she stood in the presence of her profligate and worthless son, and reminded him of the noble prophet from Judah who could interpret the message God had written on the wall. So Daniel was summoned.

Is not that a strange thing about people? We find our rightful places only in the crisis of life. At the banquet table the people are busy with the hum of conversation and the ordinary things of the day. They are talking alike, laughing alike, carrying on alike, the great, the small, the famous, the infamous, the good, the bad, all of them. But when a crisis comes, there is an unexpressed law by which men somehow take their rightful places. It is then that the man with the keys of the kingdom stands up and cries out.

It was so here in that awesome crisis at Belshazzar's feast that Daniel the prophet of God, stood up. Why, they almost had forgotten his name. You see, when Nebuchadnezzar died, his son, Evil-Merodach, took the kingdom, and reigned over it three years until the usurper, Neriglissar, murdered him. In that conspiracy the old ministers were discarded and put aside. And among them, of course, was Daniel. For a generation he had lived in obscurity. But in the great crisis, the aged prophet (he is nearing ninety years old now) was sent for, and he stood before the king.

What he said could have cost him his life. But Daniel was a prophet of God. He was sent to deliver God's message of truth. Upon this occasion he recounted to that profligate and unworthy grandson the lycanthropy of Nebuchadnezzar. Daniel reminded Belshazzar how, in that seven years of madness, Nebuchadnezzar came to acknowledge God and to make a decree for the whole world to reverence the great God of heaven. Then Daniel drove the message home to the heart of the king. "But you have sinned against light and instead of humbling yourself and following in the footsteps of your father, behold this orgy and this night of impiety and blasphemy." Did Belshazzar, in the years past, learn by the example of Nebuchadnezzar? No, he did not. When we refuse to listen to the admonitions of the Lord, when we refuse to heed the words of God, there comes an inevitable intervention from heaven. If we do not discipline ourselves, someone else will discipline us. We cannot escape. The hand of the Lord reaches and extends to the extremities of our existence. The chastening hand of God did not even wait for the sunrise. It was in the night that the hand wrote over against the wall. The feast began in mirth and revelry. It ended in a groan.

Sin somehow, always, inevitably progresses. Nebuchadnezzar will plunder and destroy in violence and war. His grandson, Belshazzar, continues in luxurious sensualism, then to voluptuous orgies, and finally to profanity and blasphemy. It is inevitable that he sees the handwriting on the wall.

Sin carries with it our own inevitable destruction. When we choose sin we choose death. James, the brother of the Lord, wrote in the first chapter of his epistle to the church at Jerusalem: "Let no man say when he is tempted, I am tempted of God: for God cannot be tempted with evil, neither tempteth he any man: But every man is tempted, when he is drawn away of his own lust, and enticed. Then when lust hath conceived, it bringeth forth sin: and sin, when it is finished, bringeth forth death" (James 1:13-15). We need no inspired eyes to see the handwriting on the wall.

FROM PAST TO PRESENT

Did this judgment happen back in some old forgotten Babylon? Yes, but it happened again last night. The past has a way of telescoping into the present. The judgments of God upon sin and excess or blasphemy fall every night, when the halls of Belshazzar are emptied and men stagger home.

> When the great factories of our cities
>   Have turned out their last finished work,
> When the merchants have sold their last yard of silk
>   And dismissed the last tired clerk;
> When the bank has racked in its last dollar
>   And paid its last dividend,
> And the Judge of the earth says "Close for the night,"
>   And asks for a balance — what then?

"But, pastor," you say, "you do not believe in that supernatural, mythological tale here of the handwriting on the wall do you?" My brother, while we are discussing the supernatural, the supernatural forces of God are molding the whole of life and existence around us. The Lord is weighing us and the Lord is judging. The Lord is decreeing, the Lord is building up, and the Lord is tearing down. We do not know who wrote the following poem, but it will do our souls good to read it again:

The Hand Upon the Wall

At the feast of Belshazzar and a thousand of his lords,
  While they drank from golden vessels, as the Book
    of Truth records,
In the night as they revelled in the royal palace hall,
  They were seized with consternation at the hand
    upon the wall.

See the brave captive Daniel as he stood before the
    throng,
  And rebuked the haughty monarch for his mighty
    deeds of wrong;
As he read out the writing, 'Twas the doom of one and
    all,
  For the kingdom was now finished, said the hand
    upon the wall.

See the faith, zeal and courage, that would dare to do
    the right,
  Which the spirit gave to Daniel this the secret of
    his might.
In his home in Judea, a captive in its hall,
  He still understood the writing of his God upon the
    wall.

So our deeds are recorded; there is a hand that's writing
    now.
  Sinner, give your heart to Jesus, to His royal mandate
    bow;
For the day is approaching, it must come to one and all,
  When the sinner's condemnation will be written on
    the wall.

Dear God, what will happen to us in the great assize when we stand at the judgment bar of Almighty God where our sins are written with the point of a diamond and incised into the very walls of eternity? We plead before God as the psalmist cried, "If thou, Lord, shouldest mark iniquities, O Lord, who shall stand?" (Ps. 130:3). Lord God, shall those rocks and mountains on which are written the records of our sins fall on us? Shall we cry in terror for the earth and the seas to hide us from the face of Him who sits on the throne and from the wrath of the Lamb? In that great day of judgment to come who shall be able to stand? Lord God, what shall happen to us?

That is why we need the Savior. That is why we need the Lord Jesus. Lord, here is a sinner man. Lord, we are sinner people. We cannot hide the gross fact from Thee. The Lord searches us and knows us. Lord, we are sinners. And what shall we do, what shall we say in the day of our appearance before Thee? Master, we need Jesus. We need God. We need the Savior. Dear God, we shall not seek to hide our iniquities from You. We are lost and undone. We need help, forgiveness, cleansing, washing, and saving. Lord, because there is no one else to turn to, we come to Thee. Who can save us? Our mothers and our fathers? My mother and my father were sinners too, and they are both dead. Those who loved me the most cannot save me. If you die before your parents do, all they can do is just bury you away out of their sight. If I die in your presence, all you can do is to bring the body of the pastor and place it on a funeral bier, and then finally lower it into the ground. Ah, how weak we are, Lord! How hopeless and how helpless we are! We are lost sinners.

But that is why Jesus came into the world. He came to die for our sins, to be raised for our justification, and someday to present us, faultless, before His great glory in heaven. That is the Gospel. That is the Evangel. That is the Good

News. God was in Christ Jesus, reconciling us to Himself, not imputing to us our sins, but bestowing upon us the glorious gift of reconciliation. We pray you therefore be ye reconciled to God. Heed the handwriting on the wall. Come to Jesus today.

THE FEAST OF BELSHAZZAR

He ended — and his passing foot was heard,
But none made answer, not a lip was stirred —
Mute the free tongue and bent the fearless brow —
The mystic letters had their meaning now!
Soon came there other sound — the clash of steel,
The heavy ringing of the iron heel —
The curse in dying, and the cry for life,
The bloody voices of the battle strife.

That night they slew him on his father's throne,
The deed unnoticed and the hand unknown;
Crownless and sceptreless Belshazzar lay,
A robe of purple, round a form of clay.
　　　　　　　　　　　　　　— *Edwin Arnold*

CHAPTER 6

WEIGHED AND FOUND WANTING

WEIGHED AND FOUND WANTING

Then was the part of the hand sent from him; and
this writing was written.

And this is the writing that was written, MENE, MENE,
TEKEL, UPHARSIN.

This is the interpretation of the thing: MENE; God
hath numbered thy kingdom, and finished it.

TEKEL; Thou art weighed in the balances, and art
found wanting.

PERES; Thy kingdom is divided, and given to the
Medes and Persians.

Then commanded Belshazzar, and they clothed Daniel with scarlet, and put a chain of gold about his neck,
and made a proclamation concerning him, that he
should be the third ruler in the kingdom. In that night
was Belshazzar the king of the Chaldeans slain.

And Darius the Median took the kingdom, being about
threescore and two years old.

Daniel 5:24-31

In our preaching through the prophet Daniel, we have
come to the conclusion of chapter 5, and I read the text:
"This is the writing that was written, MENE, MENE, TEKEL,
UPHARSIN. This is the interpretation of the thing: MENE;
God hath numbered thy kingdom, and finished it. TEKEL;
Thou art weighed in the balances, and art found wanting.

PERES; Thy kingdom is divided, and given to the Medes and the Persians" (Dan. 5:25-28).

BY WAY OF REVIEW

The kingdom of Babylonia had been invaded by the armies of Cyrus. The whole earth had fallen prey to the on-rushing armies of the Medes and the Persians. Nabonidus, son of Nebuchadnezzar and king of Babylonia, had been conquered by Cyrus and was shut up as a refugee in the city of Borsippa. Nabonidus had no particular interest in politics. He was an antiquarian, an archaeologist. Many of the records which have been preserved for us from those ancient empires of antiquity before the days of Babylon, we owe to Nabonidus. He loved to dig into the foundation of ancient ruins and finding there the records of long-lost dynasties; he would bring them to light with the stories of their kingdoms.

Nabonidus certainly was not a great soldier. Before the genius of Cyrus, who was one of the great generals of all times, Nabonidus wilted as snow melts under a burning sun. Because of his antiquarian interests, Nabonidus did not even live in Babylon. He lived in Arabia. The matters of government he left in the hands of his son, Belshazzar, a young man. But here again is an instance of something you see so often in life. There will be a fine father, a dedicated man, but his son will be profligate, sensual, carnal, and prodigal. It was so with Belshazzar. At the moment his father was fighting for his life, his kingdom and his throne, at that very moment Belshazzar called together a thousand of his sycophantic lords and shared with them a carnal orgy.

The lords are there with their concubines. They are there with their bevies of dancers. The king himself led them into desecration and blasphemy. Finally, sending to a shrine somewhere in the city where for seventy years had been kept those holy vessels which Nebuchadnezzar had taken out of the temple of Solomon, Belshazzar lifts up those holy goblets in the banquet hall to blaspheme the living God and to get inebriated by drinking wine from them. Well, as long as their tongues were loosed with wine everything was excellent. That is the way life is, you know. Eat, drink and be merry. As long as it continues, that is fine. But there is something about life that always follows a pattern of judgment.

In the midst of that orgy, there appeared a hand. The fingers of the hand wrote in the plaster on the wall, and the writing was strange. The king followed the writing of the hand. As he looked, he turned ashen and pale. His loins were loosed. His knees knocked together. He was literally terrified. The great throng of orgiastic revelers watched the eyes of the king, followed them to the writing on the wall, and then they looked back at the king to find meaning and strength. But he was more terrified than his drunken subjects. It was then that they asked for a man, any man in the kingdom, who could interpret the strange writing on the wall.

In an apartment in the palace lived the queen mother, apparently the daughter of Nebuchadnezzar. In the days of her father there had been a prophet from Judea by the name of Daniel, who had guided her father through seven years of insanity. He was a great, godly, good man. So the queen mother came before her profligate son, thinking that maybe that same seer from heaven might guide the prodigal back into a way of peace and righteousness. There Daniel was summoned. He spoke sternly, truthfully. His words were as a sword unsheathed. They were naked. They could have cost him his life. But he was a prophet of God and he delivered faithfully the message of the Lord. After his rebuke to the king, Daniel turned to the writing. "This is the writing that is written, MENE, MENE, TEKEL, UPHARSIN."

Why could not the astrologers, the Magi, the enchanters, the sorcerers, and all the king's counselors read it? Because the wisdom of this world can never comprehend the ways of God. The Book says that the wisdom of this world is foolishness with God. Paul wrote most distinctly, "For the natural man (in all his human wisdom), receiveth not the things of the spirit of God: for they are foolishness unto him: neither can he know them, because they are spiritually discerned" (I Cor. 2:14). Without the illumination of the Holy Spirit of God, no man can know the Lord. We cannot. A man by reasoning cannot find God. No philosopher, researcher, scientist, or man in his own ability, genius or endowment can come to know God. To know God is a spiritual revelation. So the wise men and the Magi and all the counselors of the king looked in bewilderment upon those strange words. They had no idea what they meant. The men of this world are never able to explain things. No man can do that. All any man can ever do is just observe what God does, the very God whom, if the man is not a Christian, he denies. The human animal cannot explain anything. He just observes it and describes it, but he cannot explain it. So the king's men look nonplussed, blank, stupid, just as mankind in itself looks, apart from the illumination of God. Without the illumination of the Spirit of the Lord, the mind of man is dark and without understanding.

The Writing Explained

As you study commentaries on this passage you will see that there are many explanations concerning why the Magi could not understand those words. Some say they were written in dark, mysterious hieroglyphics. Others say they were written in ancient Hebrew script, rather than in the Aramaic script used in the Hebrew Bible. The alphabet of the Hebrew Bible is written in square, block letters. The handwriting on Belshazzar's wall could have been written, they say, in ancient Hebrew which was before the day when they used those Aramaic alphabetical forms. However it was written, they could not understand it. But Daniel, God's man with illumination from heaven, gave the meaning. He explained it.

His interpretation is simple. "MENE, MENE, TEKEL, UPHARSIN." "MENE; God hath numbered thy kingdom, and finished it." "Mene" means "numbered." "TEKEL; Thou art weighed in the balances, and art found wanting." "Tekel" means "weighed." The next word, "Upharsin," means "division." But when Daniel comes to explain it, he says, "PERES; Thy kingdom is divided and given to the Medes and the Persians." What became of that word "Upharsin"? Well, it is the same word, but you have to see how the Hebrews will build their nomenclature.

"U" in Hebrew means "and." When the Hebrew language makes a "U" and places it in front of a word such as "divided," it means "and divided." So you may take off the "U." In Hebrew "im" or "in" is plural like "Cherub," and "Cherubim," or "Seraph," and "Seraphim." "Upharsin," is plural, so we may take off the last two letters, "in." Now you have left the basic word itself. We have taken away the first letter (meaning "and") and the last two letters also (which merely denote a plural form). Now Hebrew is written with consonants only, the basic word usually made up of three of them. In this instance the three consonants are, "P" (Pe), "R" (Resh), and "S" (Samekh). In the word "Peres" you have the same consonants: Pe, Resh, and Samekh (P, R, and S). But in Hebrew, when you put a vowel sound in front of a "P," the "P" becomes a "Ph." But when there is no vowel sound in front of it, the "P" remains a hard "P." That is why it is "Upharsin" in one place, but "Peres" in another. Now let us take these words one at a time.

NUMBERED

"Mene." Daniel said: 'This is the interpretation and meaning thereof. God hath numbered thy kingdom and finished it." Here again and once more are we introduced to one of the great revelations of God. There is a number, a measure, and a time to everything. There is a set time when you were born. There is a set time when you shall certainly die. ". . . it is appointed unto men once to die, but after this the judgment" (Heb. 9:27). Between those two set terminals, birth and death, there is a set number of days for you to live. That is why Moses says in Psalm 90, "So teach us to number our days, that we may apply our hearts unto wisdom" (verse 12). It is a foolish man who wastes time, for time is the very substance of existence. You have just so many days. They are numbered. There is an appointed time, known to God, when they shall cease. I do not care who you are, how strong you are, how well you are, where you are, when that time comes, you will certainly die.

In the book of Kings you read about Ahab. He sought to disguise himself. He put on his armor and over it he put peasant rags and then went into battle against the Syrians. There could not be any possibility of his not coming out alive. He was disguised as a harmless peasant. But Micaiah the prophet had said, "You shall surely die." As the battle raged, an archer pulled back his bow at a venture, that is, without aiming it, and let fly the arrow which entered a joint in the harness of Ahab's armor and pierced his heart, and his blood flowed out in the chariot. When that time comes you shall certainly die. "Thy kingdom is numbered and finished." "And in that night was Belshazzar the king of the Chaldeans slain." The number of his days had run out and also the number of the days of his kingdom.

There is a mystery of numbers in all God's universe. It is put together like that. All of it. What you see, the entire phenomena of life, of substance, of matter, of existence, all of it exhibits that strange creative affinity for number.

For example, matter, substance, is made up of numbers. There are a few elements, not very many. God will take a few molecules of this element, and a few molecules of that one, put them together and the result will be a substance. Change the number of those little molecules by just one, and it is an altogether different substance which results. The whole world of matter is nothing but those numerical formuli.

In the world of sound and music, numerical vibrations make the sound. A low sound does not have as many vibrations as a high sound. Increase the vibrations and higher sound results. Increase them more and more, and finally it gets beyond what the ear can hear.

Color is like that. Color is nothing but mathematical, numerical proportions. When the wave length is long and low, the colors are red. But when the wave lengths are high and short, the colors are violet. If they are too low and long, the colors are infrared and beyond our sight. If the waves are too high and short, the colors are ultraviolet and again, beyond our sight.

The whole astronomical universe is like that. You can reduce it to mathematical proportion. For many years astronomers knew that Pluto was in the universe. They had never seen it, but by mathematical law they knew it was there. Finally, a telescope was made strong enough and they could see it.

The whole universe is like that. It is numbered and we are a part of it. Those numbers are in our lives. When we come to that certain day and time, that certain number, we do not live here anymore. We are gone.

"Thy kingdom is numbered and finished." What applied to them, applies to us and to all the kingdoms of the earth. America is our nation. The sinews of America are her Christian people. The great battlements of America are her principles. The strength of America lies in her dedication to God. But when our people turn away from the Lord and give themselves to carnality, sensuality, worldliness, infidelity, and desecration, the days of America are numbered. Whether we live or whether we die, lies in the imponderables of Almighty God. "Thy kingdom is numbered and is finished."

WEIGHED

"Tekel." Daniel said, "Thou art weighed in the balances, and art found wanting." On one side God puts Himself and His Word, His revelation so plainly written. And on the other side God puts man, or the kingdom, or the church. And He weighs it. Look at what happens.

A man is weighed. On this side is God's law, God's revelation, the expectation of God. And on that side is the man. What happens to the scales? They tilt quickly. The man drops. He is found wanting. From the beginning it has been man's goal and aim and striving to pull himself up. So what does he do? For one thing he gives himself to rubrics and rituals. He observes with exact punctiliousness all of these things that pertain to formal religion. He will be baptized, he will be catechized, he will be confirmed, he will be consecrated, and he will be absolved. On Friday he will wear black and on Sunday he will wear white. He will fast while others are feasting, and he will observe those punctilious exactitudes of religion down to the finest minutia. He will try to lift himself up on the scale, in the measurement of God.

Or, if he is not of a turn to observe all of those formal exactitudes, he will give himself to moral goals and advancements. He becomes a sincere moralist, or a sincere philosopher, or a sincere speaker of the truth, or a sincere researcher. He gives himself in sincerity to the study of whatever he feels might elevate him or lift him up. As Saul of Tarsus said to the king, "King Agrippa, I verily thought within myself that I ought to do everything contrary to the name of Jesus of Nazareth" (Acts 26:9). Paul was sincere, just as sincere as he could be. But add sincerity to heresy and that does not make it orthodoxy. Sincerity alone never lifts a man up. Why? Because he needs something else. He is a fallen creature, and apart from the regenerating power of the Holy Spirit, and apart from the forgiveness, redemption, washing and cleansing in the blood of the Lamb, he cannot be saved. He cannot lift himself up by himself. He is weighed and found wanting.

A man may say, "Beginning this minute, from now on, I am going to live a perfect life and commend myself to God." I commend you for your noble resolution, but you will not take another step before you will have fallen into some kind of an error, either in thinking, or in goal, or in vision, or in ambition, or in deed. You cannot live sinlessly by yourself. And what would you do about your past sins? There is no way for a man to come up in the measure of God except as the Lord pulls him up. He cannot pull himself up. He cannot save himself.

I do not know of a better illustration of this spiritual fact than for me to come and watch you die. Let us see you save yourself. "Ah, preacher, you do not know the depths of my ability. You do not know the genius that is in my hand, and you do not know the endowment with which I can grapple with problems." Well, fine. I wish you marvelous success. But I will stand there and watch you die. You are helpless. "Ah, but pastor, you do not understand. My mother loves me and she is going to stand there by my side. My father loves me and he is going to stand there by my side. My family loves me and they are going to stand there by my side. I have influential friends and they are going to stand there by my side." Fine. When they all stand around you let them join hands. All they will do with the circle is just watch you die, and then bury you out of their sight. We are helpless. We are fallen. No man in the world can bring that scale up. You cannot be saved in yourself or through genius or love of those around you. It has to be of God. That is why the prayer of the sinner is always in order, "God in heaven be merciful to me, a sinner." God help me. If God does not help me, I am helpless. For I am weighed in the balances and found wanting.

Divided

"Peres." Daniel said, "Thy kingdom is divided, and given to the Medes and the Persians." How we try to hide ourselves from that agonizing and painful judgment! As I look around I see the whole world following that way of Belshazzar, drowning themselves in secular pleasure, unable to face the fact that they will give up all they possess to someone else someday. The world of unbelief and rejection cannot make room for that transfer. It is too awesome to face. So they give themselves to frivolity and amusement. Why, there are people who have to be entertained all the time. They could not conceive of an existence without some kind of entertainment.

In the little town in which I grew up, we did not have a radio; it had not been invented. We did not have any television; we never imagined such a thing. That was a long time ago. Maybe that is why Cris, when he was a little boy, asked me at the dinner table after church services one evening, "Daddy, did you know Noah?" I was born and raised a long time ago. We never had any automobiles; we were too poor. Nor any roads to run them on. We never had anything. But it was good for me. To this day I do not need to be entertained. I can have the best time you ever saw in your life, just by myself with God and my Bible. I can spend a day with a good book, or just talking to the Lord and thinking about the things of Jesus. I do not need to be entertained. I can live fully and wholesomely without it. Not so with this modern world. They are drowning themselves in entertainment. There are those who could not even carry on a good conversation without drugs of some kind, such as that liquid pot called liquor. The whole earth is like that. Rather than face the inevitable, they drown themselves in forgetfulness. They hide their faces.

Is not that exactly what Belshazzar was doing? His father was defeated and shut up in Borsippa. Those great walls of Babylon on every side were surrounded by the battalions of the armies of Cyrus. "Let us drown ourselves in wine and desecration and blasphemy. Let us forget it." And that night, silently, those conspirators gathered while the banquet was going on. When the orgy was at its height, they noiselessly gave a signal and the great brazen leaves of the giant, unassailable, invincible doors, the gates of Babylon, were thrown open wide and the armies of Cyrus marched in. And at that same signal, certain of those conspirators seized the Royal Palace. And *"that night"* was Belshazzar the king of the Chaldeans slain.

Herodotus, who visited Babylon city seventy years later, said that Cyrus entered it by turning the course of the Euphrates River. But commentators from the beginning have felt that Babylon really fell by treachery, by defection. In these recent years they have discovered what is called the Cylinder of Cyrus. In it Cyrus recounts how he took Babylon, and it is exactly as it is here in the Bible. In the midst of the revelry and orgy of Belshazzar, conspirators opened the gate and Cyrus marched in and took the kingdom without throwing a spear or loosing an arrow. Then that glorious head of gold found an inglorious and ignominious end. Remember Psalm 9:17, "The wicked shall be turned into hell, and all the nations that forget God." In that night Belshazzar was slain and his kingdom divided.

How infinitely better it is to face God honestly, openly. We are to remember the Scripture which says, "Neither is there any creature that is not manifest in his sight: but all things are naked and opened unto the eyes of him with whom we have to do" (Heb. 4:13). We stand before God whose eyes search our souls. "Lord, you know all about me. Master, in love and mercy remember me. Forgiveness, Lord, and understanding; how much I need it! Sympathy, Master, and redemption; give them to me else I perish. My heart needs Thee, Lord, nor can I live without Thee. Here I come, Lord. I bow in Thy presence on both knees. I humble my soul, Lord, before Thee and ask that Thou shalt extend Thy golden scepter and touch me that I might live."

Would you do that today? Would you let God lift you up in His presence? Jesus died and rose again to clothe you in robes of His righteousness without which you are weighed and found wanting. Come to Him today and let Him lift you from sin and certain doom to the heights of salvation and sure deliverance. Will you come today?

Watch and Pray

The God that stopped the sun on high
And sent the manna from the sky,
Laid flat the walls of Jericho,
And put to flight old Israel's foe;
Why can't he answer prayer today,
And drive each stormy cloud away?

Who turned the water into wine,
And healed a helpless cripple's spine,
Commanded tempest, "Peace, be still,"
And hungry multitudes did fill;
His power is just the same today,
So why not labor, watch and pray?

He conquered in the lions' den,
Brought Lazarus back to life again,
He heard Elijah's cry for rain,
And freed the sufferers from pain.
If He could do those wonders then,
Let's prove our mighty God again.

Why can't the God who raised the dead,
Gave little David Goliath's head,
Cast out the demons with a word,
Yet sees the fall of one wee bird,
Do signs and miracles today,
In that same, good, old-fashioned way?
He can! He's just the same today!

— Martin Luther

From *Sourcebook of Poetry* compiled by Al Bryant, p. 549. Copyright, 1968, by Zondervan Publishing House, Grand Rapids, Michigan.

THE GOVERNMENT OF GOD

CHAPTER 7

THE GOVERNMENT OF GOD

And Darius the Median took the kingdom, being about
threescore and two years old.   Daniel 5:31

In our preaching through the book of Daniel we come to
the end of an epoch, the end of an era. The fifth chapter of
Daniel closes with these words: "In that night was Belshazzar the king of the Chaldeans slain. And Darius the
Median took the kingdom, being about threescore and two
years old" (verses 30, 31). This message entitled, "The
Government of God," is framed in keeping with the demise
of that first great world empire. The head of gold has fallen
and never again is the seat of world government to be found
in the Mesopotamian Valley, not in the days past, nor in ages
future. It had been located there in Nineveh's Assyria and
in Babylonian Babylon for centuries. But in this little passage I have just read, the scepter passed away forever. The
transfer of power is described in one verse of just one sentence.

THE PROVIDENCE OF GOD

How rapidly do the great empires pass across the horizon
of history in the pages of the Bible! There is the empire of
the Hittites, the empires of the Egyptians, the Assyrians,
the Babylonians, the Persians, the Medians, the Greeks and

113

the Romans. The succession continues to our own day as we watch the review in modern story. The kingdoms of Spain, Germany, Austria, France, Great Britain, America, Russia, China, and Japan sweep swiftly and rapidly through the pages of history across God's horizon. But in it all the Lord reigns supreme and king forever. The sovereignty belongs to the Lord God. This is the lesson that the Lord sought to teach Nebuchadnezzar. His madness came with "the intent that the living may know that the most High ruleth in the kingdom of men, and giveth it to whosoever he will, and setteth up over it the basest of men" (Dan. 4:17b). It is God who alone reigns supreme and eternal. "God hath spoken once; twice have I heard this; that power belongeth unto God" (Ps. 62:11).

In Isaiah 40:15, we are told that in God's sight all the nations of the earth are just a drop in the bucket. Out of the depth of the well, a pail of water is drawn up. As it is lifted up, a drop falls back into the well. How inconsequential! As the pail is poured out, a drop falls by the wayside. How small and insignificant! All the nations of the world are as a drop in the bucket. Isaiah 40:15 also describes the kingdoms of the world as dust in the balance, the fine, fine dust that could not even be weighed. The whole course of human history in God's sight is as the dust in the balance. Isaiah 40:7, 8, speaks of all of the people of the world as grass. "The grass withereth, the flower fadeth." Where are the marching hosts of Nimrod and Sennacherib, of Nebuchadnezzar and Cyrus, of Xerxes and Alexander, and the legions of Caesar? Their very sons were born to bury them, as our sons and daughters are born to bury us today. The great moving mass of humanity through the centuries is like a series of fallen leaves. God alone has the overview of all meaning and purpose in history.

Our vision is so limited and circumscribed. We see so small a part of the ages. We are so insignificant and inconsequential a part of the whole. It is only God who surveys the purposes that lie back of the developments in human story. God does not deal with just one generation, but with all the previous and succeeding generations. He deals not only with this world but with the world that is to come, with all the great hosts of heaven, and with the whole infinitude of the creation of His hand. It would be only in the wisdom of an eternal overview such as this that we could ever really read the meaning of what happens, both in our lives and in the development of history.

It would be easy to imagine a fly lighting on a cornice of the great St. Paul's Cathedral in London. As he looks around and crawls on the cornice I can faintly hear him say, "What a miserable, paltry, contemptible place this is." He is not cognizant of the great overview, the dome, the pillars, and the vast proportions of that glorious house of God.

Have you been to New York City? Have you seen the Chrysler Building? To me that is one of the most beautiful edifices in America. One of the architectural monstrosities of all time is a gargoyle. But they are beautiful on the Chrysler Building. They are grotesque by themselves, but when you look at them on the Chrysler Building, they remind you of the architects in days past who invented them and used them for spouts. I can easily imagine a fly lighting on one of those gargoyles. As he crawls around it and inspects it he says: "What lack of symmetry and beauty is this? How monstrous!" From a fly's perspective he is not able to see the gorgeous, rising proportions of that glorious building. We are that way. We see so small a part until sometimes it is difficult for us to fit what we see into the great plan and purpose of God. But God sees the end from the beginning.

All the sovereign choices and decisions of God are worked out in human history. It is He and He alone who sits as Judge over all nations of the world. There are those who say that there is no meaning or purpose in history. The world came from nowhere. The world is going nowhere. It is blind and aimless. There are those who say that if there ever was a God, and if He made the universe, He wound it up and left it to its own purposes. They avow that if a being or God ever existed He has retreated from the universe and there is nothing left but what the philosophers call "second causes," and what the infidels call "blind accidents." Such is not so. The Lord lives, the Lord rules, the Lord reigns King over the nations of the earth. There is no such thing as a nation denying God, blaspheming God and continuing to live. God is active in human life and in the affairs of the nations of the earth. And the nations that forget God have in them the seeds of internal decay and destruction.

THE JUDGMENT OF GOD UPON OUR MODERN BABYLONS

The same principle of judgment we find in the life of a church and of a denomination. Wherever there is a church that forsakes the preaching of the Gospel, the winning of souls, and gives itself to rubric and ritual, God comes and takes the lamp of that church and denomination away. The whole history of Christendom is replete with one story after another of the decay and the decadence of churches and denominations. God judges the churches.

This is the same Lord God who sits in judgment upon the nations of the world. No nation continues to exist that dethrones and blasphemes God and gives itself to a carnal and sensual life. We see this judgment illustrated in the story of the capital of the Chaldeans. Babylon was built in carnality and sensuality and in the feast of Belshazzar it died never to rise again.

But let us not talk about Babylon. Let us speak about America. Let us not talk about the great city of Mesopotamia; let us talk about our great cities in the United States.

Some time ago *The Dallas Morning News* related how the mayors of America's great metropolitan areas gathered in New York City. They breakfasted at a residence for former narcotic addicts. They visited a Brooklyn Hospital where heroin addicts are treated with methadone, an addictive that is relatively harmless. Mayor Lindsay of New York said it would cost millions of dollars to rehabilitate New York's narcotic addicts who, he said, numbered about one hundred thousand. Mayor Lindsay said the drug problem could be the number one problem of America. He said: "These cities that do not have it as bad as New York, will have. They'll have it tomorrow." The mayors walked past empty shells of buildings and vacant lots littered with the rubble of buildings torn down to make room for federally-financed housing projects for which funds never became available. The visitors were shocked by the sight of the devastated area. It was Boston's Mayor Kevin White who had the final word. "This could be the first tangible sign of the collapse of our entire civilization."

This is the judgment of Almighty God. God is not dead nor has He retreated; rather He holds the nations in the balances of His hand. As in the previous chapter God weighed Babylon and its king and found both wanting. The mayor says that what has happened to New York will happen to every city in America. New York is the richest city in the richest state in the richest country that ever was. Yet it is morally and spiritually bankrupt and faces seemingly insoluble problems.

Once when I was in New York city, I listened to a TV panel involved in a discussion of the city. One of the panelists said there are two hundred thousand alcoholics in New York City. As the group continued to discuss the tragedy, another panelist said there are one million family members in New York City who are grievously affected by the two hundred thousand alcoholics. All in one, just one, American city! Mayor Lindsay says what is happening in New York will happen in every city in America. What a dismal prospect!

One of the strangest characteristics of God Almighty is that inexorable way of punishment God follows through the ages. He never changes. That inexorable way of God raises up foreign nations to punish those who defy His name. That is what happened in the days of Assyria and the northern ten tribes. Nineveh, under its kings, came down and destroyed the northern kingdom of Israel. She also shut up Judah in a vise. The great prophet Isaiah came before the Lord and asked Him why. And God replied, "O Assyrian, the rod of mine anger, and the staff in their hand is mine indignation" (Isa. 10:5). The same thing happened again when the Babylonians came and destroyed Judah and Jerusalem and Solomon's Temple. This time Habakkuk the prophet asked God why. And the Lord replied, "These bitter and hasty Chaldeans I have ordained for judgment and I have established them for correction" (Hab. 1:6a, 12b). Do not persuade yourself for a minute that God has died or retreated up there somewhere in the sky. He sits Judge of the earth.

The Russian communists have had cosmonauts flying over America. In a rendezvous they were practicing the building of space platforms up there. Do you think, do you suppose that America can give herself to desecration, drunkenness, debauchery and blasphemy and He that sitteth ruler and judge of the nations will let us escape? If God does not judge America He will have to retreat through history and apologize to Sodom, Gomorrah, Nineveh and Babylon. The same God who judged the nations of the ancient world is the Lord God who judges America today.

In the dissolution of the nations in human history, is there a kingdom that shall abide forever? Yes, there is. It is not America, it is not Russia, it is not China, as it was not

Greece, Rome, Assyria, or Babylonia, or the Hittites or the Egyptians. But there is a kingdom that shall endure through eternity. It is the kingdom of heaven, the kingdom of God. Daniel said, as he interpreted the great image and the stone cut out without hands, that like the chaff of a threshing floor the nations would be scattered away, their mighty marching armies lying in the dust of the grave. But this great stone grew until it filled all the earth. Daniel said that this stone represents the kingdom of God, the dominion of heaven, and that it abides forever and ever.

The Lord's Prayer ends with the triumphant phrase, "For thine is the kingdom and the power, and the glory, for ever. Amen." Let me read you another passage that sounds like that, in I Chronicles 29: "Thine O Lord, is the greatness, and the power, and the glory, and the victory, and the majesty: for all that is in the heaven and in the earth is thine; thine is the kingdom, O Lord, and thou art exalted as head above all. Both riches and honour come of thee, and thou reignest over all; and in thine hand is power and might" (verses 11, 12a). The government of God! I love to hear a choir sing this passage from the prophet Isaiah: "For unto us a child is born, unto us a son is given: and the government shall be upon his shoulder: and his name shall be called Wonderful, Counsellor, The mighty God, The everlasting Father, The Prince of Peace. Of the increase of his government and peace there shall be no end, upon the throne of David, and upon his kingdom, to order it, and to establish it with judgment and with justice from henceforth even for ever. The zeal of the Lord of hosts will perform this" (Isa. 9:6, 7). The kingdom of God!

QUESTIONS RAISED BY THE DOCTRINE OF THE SOVEREIGNTY OF GOD

We are now going into an altogether different area of thought. Speaking of the government of God and the sovereignty of the Lord Almighty, we come face to face with mountainous problems. To any thinking, rational person, when we speak of the eternal, immutable, unimpeachable sovereignty of God, immediately questions press into mind. Let us answer them, according to the Bible. Here is the first one.

Why the entrance of sin? If God is sovereign, if God rules over all, then why the entrance of sin? The answer lies in us. I am not free if I am not free to choose. I am an automaton if someone chooses for me. I am a mechanical contrivance. If I have personality of my own and responsibility of my own, then I must be free to choose. Let me illustrate this poignantly in the lives of you who are fathers and mothers. I speak for all of us when I say that as we watch our children grow older, O Lord, how I wish we could make the decisions for them! You see, we who are older have been at it for a long time. We have had experience. There are old heads on these shoulders and we know how things are. We see it in our own lives. But that little fellow, he does not know. He has to experience it for himself. Often I would like to make the decision for the little fellow as he grows up! But if I keep doing that, he will never stand on his own. He will never mature. He will be an emotional cripple all his life, leaning on his mother, or leaning on his father. There has to come a time when he must have the privilege of making his own mistakes. We who are parents can see the mistakes. Sometimes we weep over them. Sometimes we find our hearts broken by them, but if the child is ever to become a man or a woman, he or she must be free to make his or her own mistakes. The child must be free to choose. That is exactly what God has done with us. We are persons, just as God is, and we can choose. That is why sin came into the world. We choose to do wrong. It is a part of our being free.

Second, if God is sovereign, then why does He visit on children the sins of the fathers? Why do the successive generations bear the hurt of those who have preceded them? Why does God do that? It is because of our personalities again. We are responsible people, and the measure of every burden of that responsibility becomes increasingly apparent as we see what we are reflected in the life of the child. Oh, Lord, how it makes us pause! We are so deeply, everlastingly responsible! Why is the baby born so helpless? The period of infancy in the human species is longer than for any other kind, to cultivate in us and to teach us our accountability. This child is in my image, a part of me. My child is in my image, as I am in the image of God, and these years of feeding and nursing and caring bring that responsibility to my soul. Here again I am free. I can dash that responsibility to the ground. I can destroy it and deface it. I often think, in talking about Nebuchadnezzar, of one of his ancient Babylonian bricks. Nebuchadnezzar had a habit of putting his name on every brick made in Babylon. In the ruins of Babylon they are there by the uncounted numbers, bricks with Nebuchadnezzar's name in them. At the British museum there is a brick which has the image and name of Nebuchadnezzar impressed in it. But while it was yet soft, a dog stepped on it. And that brick, in the British Museum, has the image and name of a great king, and a dog's track over it! That is exactly what has happened to us. The image is broken and defaced. But that is a part of our human personality and freedom. We are free to step on the life of the child with a dog's track.

Third, if God is sovereign and reigns over all, then why do children die? Why do these little innocent ones suffer? That is part of the blight of this fallen race. The blight of death touches not only the flower and the fruit, but also the bud. A tragic illustration of the horror of sin is found in the illness or death of the little child. To the human philosopher sin is a light thing. All humanism is alike. All of it. It makes light of sin. Sin to the humanist is the cultural drag of our evolutionary ancestors. Sin to the humanist is just a stumbling upward. But sin is not a slight thing in the Bible. In the Word of God, sin is an awesome curse. If sin is slight, then He who could heal it is a slight Physician and Savior, the Lord Jesus. But if sin is an awesome and damnable thing that curses the race, then He who could deliver us from it can be no one but God Himself. However the humanist may present sin as a slight peccadillo, the Word of God presents it as an eternal death here and hereafter. And we see its tragedy most poignantly as it strikes the child in a broken family circle. It is the grace and love of Jesus that saves the child.

Fourth, if God is sovereign, why should the righteous suffer? Then we always have a habit of putting the other side to that question. Why do the wicked prosper? Why do God's people suffer and the wicked people prosper and live in felicity? Well, first of all, may I take a moment to point out that you should be careful in judging the so-called prosperity of the wicked. God's Word says, "The way of transgressors is hard" (Prov. 13:15b). I can spell that in many ways. The way of the transgressor is H-E-L-L. God says that the way of the transgressor is *hard*. There was a time when I looked upon the affluent and sometimes famous as seemingly so happy. I would think, *How happy they are, how blessed they are, and how glad their days!* Then as I came to know some of these people intimately, I found that what looked like happiness from without was really hell within. There is no exception to it. If there is an exception to it, then God does not live. A man cannot live in sin and in gross carnality and in rejection of God and in unbelief and atheism and be happy. He cannot. Inside that man is a misery that is unspeakable. That goes for the whole human race and for all the nations of the earth. When carnality, sensuality, debauchery, atheism, and rejection of God swept over France in the 1700's, it swept over England in the same century. But the nations turned two different ways. Satan bathed France in a godless bloodbath, but John and Charles Wesley preached the Gospel and brought to England a national revival. Do not persuade yourself that the wicked prosper. Their way is hard.

But why do the righteous suffer? We just do not see all of God's purposes of grace. Our vision is so limited. Let me illustrate that from the Book. Do you remember when the sons of Jacob came to their father and laid before him Joseph's coat of many colors? They had sold the boy to the Ishmaelites who took him down into Egypt and auctioned him off on a slave block. To hide their monstrous crime, the brothers took Joseph's coat of many colors and dipped it in the blood of a goat, of a kid, and laid it before Israel and said: "Is not this the coat of your son Joseph? Is not this the coat of the many colors? Look at the stains of blood. Something terrible has happened to him." Jacob picked up the blood-stained coat and said: "It is my son's coat. I will go down into the grave unto my son mourning" (Gen. 37:35b). Later he said something else. Do you remember that? "All these things are against me" (Gen. 42:36). "All of these things are against me," said Israel in his grief. Let us now turn the pages of the Bible. Do you remember what Joseph said to his brothers when they came and were saved out of a devastating famine? Joseph said, "God meant it unto good" (Gen. 50:20b). Is not that what the Book says? His brothers meant it for evil, but God meant it for good. All these tragedies that overwhelm us, seem so tragic and so awesome. But God, in His great overview, means it for good. "It is good for me," said the psalmist, "that I have been afflicted" (Ps. 119:71a). The Lord refused to remove Paul's thorn in the flesh, saying, "My grace is sufficient for thee: for my strength is made perfect in weakness." And Paul said, "Therefore I take pleasure in infirmities, in reproaches, in necessities, in persecutions, in distresses for Christ's sake: for when I am weak, then am I strong" (II Cor. 12: 9, 10).

THE REIGN OF GOD

God takes the deeds of evil men and He turns them to His glory. Do not be filled with anxiety about evil men. They are not able to divert or to interdict the holy purposes of God. In Simon Peter's sermon at Pentecost recorded in the book of Acts is an astonishing verse about Jesus. "Him, being delivered by the determinate council and foreknowledge of God, ye have taken, and by wicked hands have crucified and slain" (Acts 2:23). The most dastardly deed any power or government or rulers of men ever committed was to take the gentle Jesus and crucify Him. But Simon Peter says the tragedy happened according to the determinate counsel and foreknowledge of God. God knew all about it, and He turned that tragic hour to the saving of the world.

The unchanging ways of God do not deny His existence or prove His retreat from the earth, but they rather confirm our confidence and our assurance in Him. What God says and does and ordains we can stand by forever, for God is unchangeable. He is immutable and unimpeachable. The sureness of God's laws speaks of a marvelous confidence we can have in Him. What if the sea were sometimes liquid and sometimes solid? What if things sometimes fell up, sometimes fell down, and sometimes fell to the side? What if winter and summer were irregular and you could not tell when the seasons might come? The fixedness of God's immutable laws speaks of the immutability of God. We can have confidence in Him. He is the Lord. He rides in the trickle of the little stream as well as on the bosom of the great sea. He is in the atom as He is in the fixed stars. He is today as He was yesterday and forever. We can have confidence and assurance in God.

In the sovereign purposes of God, He has given to us the kingdom. And all that happens, all of it, every headline of every paper, every page of every book of history, and every incident in your life and in the development of the world, all of it, is for you. He is getting us ready for that great, glorious consummation of the age when we shall inherit the kingdom. Paul says in Romans 8, "For ye have not received the spirit of bondage again to fear." Does what happens in history, what happens in death, and what happens in life, bring stark, terrorizing terror to us? No! We have not received the Spirit of fear. Not we. "But ye have received the spirit of adoption, whereby we cry, Abba, Father. . . . And if children, then heirs; heirs of God, and joint-heirs with Christ" (verses 15, 17). What does that mean? It means this and this triumphantly. When we get to glory, when we walk down those golden streets, when we appear before the Judge of all people, we will not appear before God as a forgiven criminal who barely is tolerated in the presence of the Judge who sentenced Him. It will not be that way at all. Rather, when we stand before the Judge of all the earth, we will be received and welcomed as sons of the Father. We will come not as a criminal the judge tolerates, but as a son the Lord loves.

The redeemed are washed, cleansed, reconciled, forgiven, and welcomed into the household of the Savior. That is what God proposes for us. Ah, dear fellow travelers, lift up your heads. Raise your eyes. Look to heaven. It is glory every step of the way. God still reigns with Christ of the kingdom and He has made us heirs.

HYMN OF TRUST

O Love Divine, that stooped to share
    Our sharpest pang, our bitterest tear,
On Thee we cast each earth-born care,
    We smile at pain while Thou art near!

Though long the weary way we tread,
    And sorrow crown each lingering year,
No path we shun, no darkness dread,
    Our hearts still whispering, Thou art near!

When drooping pleasure turns to grief,
    And trembling faith is changed to fear,
The murmuring wind, the quivering leaf,
    Shall softly tell us, Thou art near!

On Thee we fling our burdening woe,
    O Love Divine, forever dear,
Content to suffer while we know,
    Living and dying, Thou art near!

— Oliver Wendell Holmes

THE SUPERLATIVE MINISTER

CHAPTER 8

THE SUPERLATIVE MINISTER

It pleased Darius to set over the kingdom an hundred and twenty princes, which should be over the whole kingdom;

And over these three presidents; of whom Daniel was first: that the princes might give accounts unto them, and the king should have no damage.

Then this Daniel was preferred above the presidents and princes, because an excellent spirit was in him; and the king thought to set him over the whole realm.

Then the presidents and princes sought to find occasion against Daniel concerning the kingdom; but they could find none occasion nor fault; forasmuch as he was faithful, neither was there any error or fault found in him.

Then said these men, We shall not find any occasion against this Daniel, except we find it against him concerning the law of his God.

Then these presidents and princes assembled together to the king, and said thus unto him, King Darius, live for ever.

All the presidents of the kingdom, the governors, and the princes, the counsellors, and the captains, have consulted together to establish a royal statute, and to make a firm decree, that whosoever shall ask a petition of any God or man for thirty days, save of thee, O king, he shall be cast into the den of lions.

Now, O king, establish the decree, and sign the writing, that it be not changed, according to the law of the Medes and Persians, which altereth not.

Wherefore king Darius signed the writing and the decree.

Now when Daniel knew that the writing was signed, he went into his house; and his windows being open in his chamber toward Jerusalem, he kneeled upon his knees three times a day, and prayed, and gave thanks before his God, as he did aforetime.

Then these men assembled, and found Daniel praying and making supplication before his God.

Daniel 6:1-11

By the title, "The Superlative Minister," we mean the minister of state, the greatest prime minister who ever lived, the prophet-statesman Daniel. In the previous chapter we discussed the close of an epoch and an era, that of the golden head, the first great world empire of the times of the Gentiles, the kingdom of Babylon. It is now gone forever. The golden head has fallen, and the breast of silver, with its arms of Media and Persia, now reigns supreme in the earth. But this Daniel — holy, saintly man of God — continues in power, in grace, in glory, and in gracious acceptance.

THE PLACE OF PROMINENCE

The story of Daniel and the lions' den begins with the kingly exaltation and choice of Daniel. "And over these three presidents; of whom Daniel was first" (Dan. 6:2). That is the key to all that follows after. We are so caught up in the vivid, bristling, fast-moving narrative until we overlook this foundational presentation. We are so overwhelmed by the lions' den and the guardian angel, by the night of agony and watchfulness, and by the retribution of Daniel's enemies, that we do not notice this sentence which is the basis of all that follows. But look at it carefully, "of whom Daniel was first."

In the story of Saul, the king of Israel, and David, the shepherd boy, everything is beautiful and fine, going along wonderfully well, until Saul heard the women singing about the defeat of the armies of Philistia by young David. When Saul heard the women of Israel singing, "Saul hath slain his thousands, and David his ten thousands" (I Sam. 18:7), it was a new day and a different story. On that day Saul turned against David. Jealousy destroyed his heart. It was no less true here. When Daniel was elevated to first place in the cabinet of ministers, his doom was sealed.

Daniel was truly first. He was first in the eyes of the people. He led a noble, pure life of dedication and integrity. You cannot hide a city set on a hill, nor can you hide a noble, worthy, steadfast, Christian life. This Daniel was first, manifestly so, overtly so, in the eyes of the people.

He was first also in the eyes of the new king. The king was looking for a man of integrity to be prime minister and head of state, and he found every worthy endowment in this Daniel. So the king sought to set Daniel high above all the rulers and princes in the realm. Now "this Daniel was preferred above the presidents and princes." That word "preferred" in the original Aramaic, has in it a meaning, "he outshown them all." There was a light in Daniel not found in the other counselors and cabinet members. It was as though he were inspired. His judgment was as though a man had inquired at an oracle of God. His words were like music, as though they came from a heavenly height, and his syllables were full of glory, as though the Lord God was speaking through him. This Daniel was preferred. He outshown the rest. There was a light in him. There was a charismatic grace about him.

There was a spirit of divinity in Daniel, a heavenly quickening. He was preferred above the presidents and the princes because of an excellent spirit within him (Dan. 6:3). God saw it. He inspired the writing of the story. Three times in the book of Daniel is the prophet called, "the beloved." God called him that. In the book of Ezekiel, the Lord names three great men, Noah first, Job third, and Daniel in the middle: Noah, Daniel, Job. Daniel was a contemporary of Ezekiel, and yet the inspired prophet Ezekiel saw in Daniel that excellent spirit so as to think of him alongside the ancient greats. As I read the Bible, there are three wonderfully noble, pure, saintly, godly men in the Old Testament. One is Joseph. There was never a fault in him. Another is Jonathan, the pure, magnanimous, handsome, loving Jonathan, the friend of David. And the third is Daniel.

An Excellent Spirit

There is an excellent spirit in Daniel. God saw it, and said so. The king saw it and said so. The king was aware of all of those gracious, noble statesman-like ministries of Daniel in the days gone by, as he stood before Nebuchadnezzar outlining the course of Babylon's history (Dan. 2), and as he stood in the presence of the people of the empire, guiding the realm of the Chaldeans during those seven years that the king was insane (Dan. 4). In the fifth chapter of the book Daniel is faithfully presenting the message of wisdom before Belshazzar, the degenerate, unworthy, and debauched grandson of Nebuchadnezzar, in whose life the kingdom died. Every detail in the life of Daniel confirmed him as a faithful counselor and a true friend. It is not surprising, therefore, that King Darius found in him that same glorious endowment, "an excellent spirit."

We today, no less than they of the long ago, can see that excellent spirit in the noble prophet. As I read the life of Daniel, I feel the quickening uplift of this saintly, holy and godly man. "For there was found in him an excellent spirit." Look at him for just a moment. How old was he? Let us add it up. He was born about 625 B.C. When Cyrus, with the Medes and Persians, took over the kingdom, it was 537 B.C. So if Daniel was born about 625 B.C., and this happened about 537 B.C., then Daniel was about eighty-eight years of age when he stood before King Darius. I would say that any man nearly ninety years of age is a candidate for decrepitude. He frequently is living in the past. He often is patting his great, great grandchildren on the head and telling them about the good old days. But not Daniel. It is summertime in his heart. There is godwardness in his soul. There is a moving, quickening uplift about the man, even though he is almost ninety years of age. There is a youthfulness about him. There is a hopefulness about him. There is a spirit of optimism about him, and it is contagious. This Daniel, almost ninety years of age, is still in soul and in spirit, living the life of a young man. His days are filled with intense activity. Though old in body, he is young in being.

The prince of preachers and man of God, Dr. Robert G. Lee, was asked on his eighty-fourth birthday (11 November 1970), "Are you going to keep on preaching after 84?" He answered in typical Lee language and spirit:

> When there are so many unsaved people around, when there are sorrowing hearts to be comforted, when so many young people are throwing away in Folly's Court and Carnal Pleasure's Mart the wealth God gave them at the start, when there are so many evils against which protest must be made, when so many old people are lonely on the Sunset Trail, when, in 1910 at my ordination, I was married to preaching until death do us part — why should I not, in the 85th year of life, keep on preaching?

Dr. Lee then added some fortifying statistics that ought to bless and encourage any man who is nearing the sunset days of his life. Look at his words:

> Newman Darland, a scholar of accepted standing, made an analysis of the lives and achievements of 400 foremost characters of history. The analysis showed that nearly 80 percent of the world's greatest figures closed active lives

between 58 and 80; 25 percent continuing beyond 70; 22½ percent beyond 80 and 6 percent beyond 90.

Consider what has been done by men beyond 80:

When 83, Gladstone, for the fourth time, became Prime Minister of Great Britain. Michaelangelo at 89 executed his "Last Judgment" — perhaps the most famous single picture in the world.

John Wesley preached with almost undiminished eloquence at 88 — closing at that remarkable age the most remarkable career of his time, traveling 250,000 miles in an age that knew neither electricity nor steam, delivered 4,000 sermons, wrote hundreds of volumes.

Edison was still inventing at 90. Wright, at 90, was considered a most creative architect. Shaw was still writing plays at 90. Grandma Moses began painting at 79. J. C. Penney, great Christian, was working strenuously at his business at 95.

Upon the occasion of the fiftieth reunion of his old classmates at Bowdoin College, Henry Wadsworth Longfellow penned these famous and encouraging lines from his poem, "MORITURI SALUTAMUS":

But why, you ask me, should this tale be told
To men grown old, or who are growing old?
It is too late! Ah, nothing is too late,
Till the tired heart shall cease to palpitate.
Cato learned Greek at eighty; Sophocles
Wrote his grand Oedipus, and Simonides
Bore off the prize of verse from his compeers,
When each had numbered more than fourscore years,
And Theophrastus, at fourscore and ten,
Had but begun his "Characters of Men."
Chaucer, at Woodstock with the nightingales,
At sixty wrote the Canterbury Tales;
Goethe at Weimar, toiling to the last,
Completed Faust when eighty years were past.
These are indeed exceptions; but they show
How far the gulf-stream of our youth may flow
Into the arctic regions of our lives,
Where little else than life itself survives.

How do you like that? Think of the years that lie ahead for those of us on the leeward side! Our best and our finest years are ahead.

But let us look at Daniel once again. You will never find a flaw in his life or attitude. He does not complain. In all these chapters, in all these words, there is never even an approach to a complaint. Not one. He is a captive. He is a slave. He is a trophy of war. He is one of the spoils of battle, uprooted out of his home, carried off to a strange and alien land, made a slave in the court, yet he never utters a word of complaint. His spirit is free. His soul is unfettered. His thoughts are Godward and he lives the life of a triumphant man.

That is what it is to be a Christian. How many dungeons, how many rocks, and how many dens and dives have heard the singing of God's saints that the lofty cathedral has never heard? How many of these humble disciples of Jesus who were oppressed, persecuted, and cast out as the scum of the earth have in their angelic devotion taken wings to soar into the very heaven of heavens? Daniel was like that. He was an alien in a foreign country, but he lived the victorious life of a pilgrim journeying toward the Promised Land.

There is another facet of Daniel's life that beautifully portrays his excellent spirit. It is to be found in a tragedy that accompanied his enforced slavery. According to the prophecy of Isaiah, he was probably a eunuch. When Merodach-Baladan was king of Babylon, he sent an emissary to Hezekiah to woo him away from Assyria. And Hezekiah was, oh, so complimented. His vanity was so pleased that he should thus be honored by an emissary from Babylon. But God sent Isaiah to Hezekiah, and Isaiah said: "Behold, the days come, that all that is in thine house, and that which thy fathers have laid up in store until this day, shall be carried to Babylon: nothing shall be left, saith the Lord. And of thy sons that shall issue from thee, which thou shalt beget, shall they take away; and they shall be eunuchs in the palace of the king of Babylon" (Isa. 39: 6, 7). Now the book expressly says that Daniel was of the seed royal. And in 605 B.C., when Nebuchadnezzar besieged Jerusalem and took it for the first time, he took away some of the household of the king. One of them was Daniel. By the prophecy, therefore, I think Daniel was made a eunuch. Do you ever find his complaint about being an emasculated man, a dry branch, without hope of issue or offspring? Do you? No.

There was found in this Daniel an excellent spirit. He was always looking Godward, always filled with hope, optimism, and persuasion of things glorious yet to come. An excellent spirit always typifies the man of God. To real Christians, trials, tribulations, and the sorrows of life but make them shine the brighter, like polishing a mirror. Romans 5:3 says, ". . . we glory in tribulation also." A Christian like that is an ornament of the earth and the beauty of heaven. "There was found in him an excellent spirit." I am particularly sensitive to that, because I find among people (and I fall into it every once in a while) the spirit of complaint. Complaining people rub off on me something unpleasant, something I do not want. When I am around them, I feel down. But read about Daniel, and you feel up. Whatever our darkened circumstances, there is some better thing God is preparing for us who love Him.

THE PRICE OF PROMINENCE

Now I wish I could leave this part of the sermon out, but I cannot because it is a part of human life. Whenever a man is lifted by the Lord to a place of prominence, he pays a price. There are those who seek to destroy him. In his exaltation the envious, diabolical plan to destroy this detested Daniel was born. All exaltation and all success carries with it those same working principles.

Let us speak first of the price the man pays for success in itself. There is no exaltation, no success, no prominence not paid for in slavery. The man who succeeds is a man who works, who labors. He is a slave. He is chained. Is he a musician? Then he is fastened to the piano, to the keyboard, to the organ. If he excells, if he is good, he spends untold hours at his task. Is he an artist? Is he an author? A poet? Is he a physician? Is he a theologian? If he excells, he pays for his advancement. He slaves at his assignment. He pours his life into his work.

Think also of the responsibility that comes with it. A powerful man is the president of the United States. President Nixon says: "Many times I take five minutes for lunch. Many times I take five minutes for dinner." Sitting by his side, eating dinner in the State Department Building, I was most attentive when he said to me, "I see the President with his coat off and his sleeves rolled up, working far into the wee hours of the night." Responsibility goes with success. These who are cheaply and falsely ambitious covet the honors, but they shun the sacrifice and the slavery. All prominence costs. If there is exaltation, there is payment for it. It is wonderful to be exalted, but the responsibility which comes with that prominence is laborious. It is heavy and awesome. Joseph was exalted, but on him fell the responsibility of state.

Another bitter concomitant of greatness is that it is dogged, hounded and followed by envy. The souls of many burn in rage against a great man though he has done them no injury and no harm. And the more successful a man is, the more exalted he is, the more he is despised. Nor is goodness any deterrent. Hate this Daniel? Despise this saintly and holy man? He is an old man. He is a slave. He is a captive. He does not deserve hate. But because he is exalted, he is hated. That is human nature.

Do you remember what Plato once said? Plato said that

if truth were to come down from heaven and walk on the earth, she would be so lovely and desirable the whole world of men would fall down and worship before her. But that idealistic assumption of Plato is denied by both secular and sacred history. Truth did come down from heaven. "I am 'he aletheia,' the truth" (John 14:6). Truth did come down from heaven, and what did men do? They said: "Crucify Him. Crucify Him. Away with Him." They said, "Not this man, but Barabbas." And Barabbas was a murderer, an insurrectionist, a robber. Truth did come down. This mistaken philosophy of Plato is but one more of the endless, interminable illustrations and instances of the attitude of human philosophy toward sin. To the philosophers, sin is a slight thing. It is just a cultural drag out of which we shall evolve someday. But according to God, sin has occasioned the fall of the entire human soul. It is a dark, disastrous curse according to the revealed Word of God. Sin has entered our minds and our souls, our hearts, our imagination, our dreams, our lives, and our deeds. We are a fallen people. I do not know of a more poignant illustration of the dark penetrations of sin than this found in the lives of these conspirators against Daniel. They hate this good man. They envy this saintly man. They seek the destruction of Daniel.

Jealousy is an awesome thing. It destroys wherever it touches. The most tragic part of envy and jealousy, as vile and hurtful as it is against these of whom we are envious, is its destructive power in our own hearts. Jealousy has a devastating effect upon us. It is an undercutting of human personality. When others are praised we close our ears. If something nice is said, we turn away. We are envious. We are jealous. Oh, may God deliver us from such littleness!

In London, contemporary with young Charles H. Spurgeon, was an older preacher who had been in the city for a generation. This young man, Charles Spurgeon, came to London when he was about twenty years of age. Immediately (I do not mean in a year or two or three, but immediately), there could not be found an area large enough to hold the people who wanted to hear him preach. He was like a star, like a galaxy that appeared in the sky. The older minister said that when the throngs began to crowd around the young man, envy and jealousy entered his heart and ate him up. There he was, a famous preacher in London, but the throngs were listening to Charles Haddon Spurgeon. The older pastor said he got down on his knees and cried out before God. He told the Lord all about it. Then he said the Lord began to put into his heart praise and intercession and pleading for the young man, Spurgeon. He said: "The day came after I prayed and took it to God, when upon every victory Spurgeon won, I felt as though I had done it myself. I had so prayed for him and so asked God to bless him, that when the awards and the exaltations and the throngs and the souls came to the young man, I just felt as though I had done it myself. I rejoiced and was glad." That is a Christian.

Envy and jealousy burned in the souls of these presidents, princes, governors, captains, and counselors against Daniel, for they were not "Christians." So they said, "Do away with him." That is the only answer the pagan has against the saints of God. "Do away with them. Burn them at stakes. Drown them in water. Let them rot in dungeons. Cut their tongues out. Hang them." Paganism has no other answer. How does communism confront Christian people except by fire and flame and prison? They do not have any other answer. They are godless. They are pagan. They are heathen. There is no answer on the part of heathenism except to destroy and to persecute.

But how do you do away with this Daniel? "First," they said, "Let us test everything that he does in the kingdom to see if we can find a flaw in him." And they did just that. Every judgment he made, every deed he did, every mandate he signed, every order he gave as he governed the kingdom, was carefully scrutinized by his enemies. But they found in him no fault at all. It was as if God, Himself, were directing the affairs of this Daniel. He dispensed patronage with absolute impartiality. He was above bribery. There is not anything in public office so vile and so vicious as a politician who has his hand in the till. All you have to do is read the daily newspapers to see how the politician enriches himself with his hand underneath the table. Had Daniel been open to bribe, had he one eye open as he held the scales of balance and justice, had he closed his mouth when he should be speaking out, had there been any fault in him, they would have seized upon it immediately. But he was impeccable. He was uncorruptible. He was a man of integrity, honesty, nobility, and purity. Try as they could, they could find no occasion for fault in him. Don't you wish you could vote for a man like that?

But the conspirators looked more closely at Daniel. They said to one another: "Have you noticed the God he worships? He does not worship idols. And when we have this grand march in honor of Bel-Merodach, and when we go through all the ceremonies, genuflections, incense burning and adorations before our idols, do you notice Daniel does not take part? Do you notice he talks to someone he calls Jehovah, the Lord God, and he communes with Him? Do you notice that? That is our clue. That is our open door. We will accuse Him of worshiping his God." And what a diabolical scheme they concocted!

The text of the story says, "Then these presidents and princes assembled together to the king." The original Aramaic of the text suggests that "they tempestuously, tumultuously, ran into the presence of the king." They forgot all the etiquette of the Medes and the Persians. It was as though they had been suddenly inspired by a mighty impulse. They just rushed into the presence of the king. The king did not realize that their haste was premeditated and planned. What they did appeared to be impulsively done. It seemed to be something that just rose up in their hearts as they thought on the glory and greatness of King Darius. They impulsively, impetuously, tumultuously rushed into his presence and said: "O king, we have had a divine inspiration. What we want to do is to make you god for a month." He was immediately caught like a fly in a web. How stupid can a king get? "We are going to make you god for a month." Were any of you women ever candidates for "Queen for a Day"? Were you? Well, this is "God for a Month." "We'll elect you president of the whole universe, and no subject in the whole realm is to kneel before any god or make any petition except to thee, O king. We are going to pray toward thee. We're going to lift up our hands of supplication to thee. We're going to bow down in adoration to thee. You are going to be god, divine and infallible, for thirty days." Whether they intended a lunar month or a calendar month I do not know. But what I do know is that the king was flattered. Had he reflected upon it, had there been time for argument, he would have remembered that there were three presidents, and only two of them were there. Daniel was missing. Had the king even thought, he never would have fallen into such a ghastly trap. But it was done tumultuously. They rushed into his presence as though they had divine inspiration, as if they were filled with impulsive love and appreciation for their great king. And without thinking, he signed the decree. Just like that (in the time of the snapping of the fingers), he signed it.

Standing Unperturbed

"And when Daniel knew that the writing was signed," this sedate, stately, holy, godly man walked on unperturbed in quiet assurance and self-possession. Whether the world noticed or not, Daniel did not change. He walked before God in quiet peace and self-assurance.

On the fourth floor of one of our buildings there is a famous picture of Daniel. I have seen copies of it in one place or another ever since I was a little boy. I looked at it yesterday again. Daniel is standing there with his hands behind his back, standing in quiet contemplation with the lions looking at him in awe and wonder. Well did the prophet Isaiah say, "Thou will keep him in perfect peace, whose mind is stayed on thee" (Isa. 26:3).

When Daniel knew of the writing, and that it was signed, he remained just the same — unperturbed, without anxiety or foreboding, just standing in the presence of the great God. As I think of this aged man, I think of aged Polycarp. When they burned Polycarp at the stake in Smyrna in A.D. 155, he had been a Christian for eighty-six years. Before they lit the fire they called on Polycarp to deny the Lord and save his life. In quiet assurance and with steady voice he said: "Eighty and six years have I served Him, and He hath done me no harm. Why should I forsake Him now?" And Polycarp, disciple of John, with praises on his lips, in quiet commitment to the Lord, looked at those flames as but a chariot of fire to waft his soul up to heaven. I think of Simon Peter in Acts 12, awaiting the next morning when Herod Agrippa was to cut off his head. An angel came to deliver him, but Simon Peter was sound asleep, chained between two Roman soldiers. He was sound asleep on the eve of his execution. "Thou wilt keep him in perfect peace, whose mind is stayed on thee."

Lord, how many times do I find myself perplexed, full of anxiety, disturbed and perturbed, so fearful and foreboding? Lord, take it away. May I walk through the days of the years of my life, with my face upward, and my heart quiet in the grace and goodness and mercy of God. God make me like Daniel, steady, quiet, assured, standing for Thee. Lord,

You can do that for me through Jesus. What He endured for me can make me strong to endure for Him. Here I am, Lord. Though all others turn against me, Yet may I stand with Thee. Take my heart, Lord. Take my life, blessed Jesus. Like Daniel, I give myself to You, now and forever.

Daniel

Imperial Persia bowed to his wise sway —
    A hundred provinces his daily care;
A queenly city with its gardens fair
    Smiled round him — but his heart was far away.
Forsaking pomp and power "three times a day"
    For chamber lone, he seeks his solace there:
    Through windows opening westward floats his prayer
Toward the dear distance where Jerusalem lay.
So let me morn, noon, evening, steal aside
    And shutting my heart's door to earth's vain pleasure
    And manifold solicitudes, find leisure;
The windows of my soul to open wide
    Toward that blest city and that heavenly treasure
Which past these visible horizons hide.

                  — *Richard Wilson*

WINDOWS OPENED TOWARD HEAVEN

CHAPTER 9

WINDOWS OPENED TOWARD HEAVEN

> Now when Daniel knew that the writing was signed,
> he went into his house; and his windows being open
> in his chamber toward Jerusalem, he kneeled upon his
> knees three times a day, and prayed, and gave thanks
> before his God, as he did aforetime.
>
> Daniel 6:10

In our preaching through the book of Daniel we have
come to one of the golden incidents to be found in the Word
of God. The devil's dark, devious devices and designs seemingly spell death for the holy man of God, but he faithfully
serves his Lord just the same.

THE EVIL PLOT

What had happened? The conspirators in the court of
Darius, moved with envy and personal ambition, sought the
destruction of Daniel, the holy man of God. They searched
every area of his life to find some fault of which they could
accuse him. But his life was impeccable. His political administration of government as minister of state was faultless. He was noble, steadfast, and faithful. In despair they
said to one another, "There is no fault in this man. We can
find nothing whereby to accuse him to the king."

But the devil is full of subtlety and has an endless series

147

of devious devices. He whispered in the ears of those presidents, governors, princes, and conspirators. He said to them: "How stupid can you be? Have you looked at this Daniel? Have you noticed his eccentric faith? He passes by your idol temples in silent scorn. He has no veneration for your divinities. He does not share in those genuflections, worshipings, and adorations of gods and goddesses. Haven't you noticed that?"

And the conspirators said to Satan: "Yes, that is obvious. But how can we find fault with him to accuse him in that?"

Satan whispered back and said: "Are you so artless as not to notice that the man is very religious, that he steadfastly prays to an unseen God? I know his faithful devotion. I have enticed him with every reward of social preferment, but he would rather die than fail his God. You can trap that man in his devotion to his God through prayer. You are sure to do it, because he is sure to pray."

And the conspirators whispered back to Satan, "But how do we find fault to accuse a man because he prays?"

Satan whispered back into their hearts: "You are looking at the wrong man. You are looking at the strength of Daniel. Look at the king. Every man has a chink in his armor. Every man has a weakness in his life. Look at the king. I know him. He is subject to vanity and to flattery. Make him god for a month. Pass a law honoring him which declares that, for a month, no one is to pray to any god except to the king. Then you will trap that Daniel like an eagle pulled down out of the sky."

That is Satan. He knows our strength and works day and night to cut, to sever, that cord that binds us to the unseen and eternal God.

What Shall He Do?

When Daniel knew that the writing was signed, making it a penalty of sure death to pray to anyone but the king, what did he do? He could have sat down in the chair in his house and thought within himself: *How shall I circumvent these devils? I know. I will fight cunning with cunning, craft with craft. I will concoct a scheme that will frustrate their evil designs. I know what I shall do. I shall go before the king myself and uncover before his eyes their murderous plot. I will call an assembly of all the statesmen and all the leaders of the Babylonian government, and I will accuse these designers and deceivers to their face. That is what I will do.*

What could Daniel have done? He could have temporized, that is, argued with his conscience. "The law said just thirty days. Well, we will just postpone the prayer meetings for thirty days." Or he could have said: "My life is worth more to my people than my death. I ought to stay alive for the sake of my countrymen who are in captivity." He could have said: "I will keep the king from doing a murderous deed. I will foil the schemes of my enemies. I will be astute in this and give no occasion for accusation against me." Or he could have said: "The end justifies the means. I will just shut the window when I pray. They will not know that I pray. I can pray in my heart. God searches the heart. He knows that I am praying. I do not have to pray in that little chapel with the open window. I can pray in some other room in my house. I can pray in the cellar and the king will not know it. I can live like a heathen though I am really a believer. I will just hide my face out of sight for thirty days and they will not know but that I am as godless and idolatrous as any circumspect Babylonian who ever walked through the king's court."

Is not that a strange thing about the Lord God? It is part of His character. There is something in God that asks us to be open, public, and unashamed in our devotion, religious practice, and commitment. In the night of the Passover, the blood had to be displayed openly on the front of the house in the sign of the cross, above the door and on either side. Why should not the blood have been sprinkled on the back door, or in a closet? Because God said, "My people are to be openly and unashamedly committed." There is no exception to that in the whole Word of the Lord. "Who is on the Lord's side? Let him come unto me," cried Moses (Exod. 32:26). And the Lord Himself said, "Whosoever shall deny me before men, him will I also deny before my Father which is in heaven" (Matt. 10:33). In Romans 10:9, Paul says, "If thou shalt confess with thy mouth the Lord Jesus . . . thou shalt be saved." There is public prayer as well as private prayer. There is public reading of the Word of God as well as private reading. There is public worship of the Lord God as there is private worship of the Lord.

The Open Window

Daniel could have temporized. "I will just hide my face out of sight until the storm is passed." But no! "Now when Daniel knew that the writing was signed, he went into his house; and his windows being open in his chamber toward Jerusalem, he kneeled upon his knees three times a day, and prayed, and gave thanks before his God, as he did aforetime" (Dan. 6:10). Whether they noticed it or not, whether they approved or disapproved, Daniel went on his way serving God as he had before. Just as the sun rises and shines, whether men notice it or not; just as the sea rolls in majestic tranquillity, whether men observe it or not; just as the mighty mountain peaks rear their heads in snowy grandeur to the azure blue of the sky, whether anyone sees them or not; just as the stars in their orbits swing around these suns in their universes, whether men chart their courses or not; so a man of a great, majestic, mighty spirit serves God, whether anyone approves or disapproves, whether anyone notices or not. He goes right on his way. I think it would have been the same had Darius made a public proclamation that he was abdicating his throne and was bestowing his crown upon Daniel. It would have made no difference in the man. He would have continued on in his worship of God just the same. Daniel would have prayed three times a day just the same. Whether in honor or in reproach, Daniel was serving God, not for the approbation or approval of men, but because of the Lord God.

I would like to pause right here and say something to myself. "Lord, I would like to learn that. When men attack the Bible, let us just go right on; let us publish another and a new edition of two million copies. When men storm through the schools of Christendom in liberalism and modernism and unbelief, let us just organize a Bible institute. When the blasphemers and the scorners seek to make us look ridiculous as though we were half insane or certainly medieval, let us just believe God all the more and preach this Book more fervently and earnestly. Let us just go right ahead. Let us just go right on."

"And when Daniel knew that the writing was signed, he went into his house; and his windows being open in his chamber toward Jerusalem, he kneeled down upon his knees three times a day, and prayed, and gave thanks to his God, as he did aforetime." That is Daniel.

I think of Nehemiah in the sixth chapter of his book. When Sanballat and Tobiah sought to intimidate him, Nehemiah sent word to them and said: "Should such a man as I flee?" (Neh. 6:11). Should a man who serves God be a craven coward? Daniel is like Nehemiah. He is absolutely fearless and absolutely not to be turned aside from his commitment to God. The whole empire may go wrong but Daniel does not go wrong. The king may go wrong but Daniel does not go wrong. The people may go wrong but Daniel does not go wrong. I can imagine as he went to his house (and it pointedly states in the text that when he knew the writing was signed he went into his house), climbing the steps of his house was like ascending the steps of a gallows. But he is at peace. His life is in the hands of the Lord. Whether to live, whether to die, whether to be fed to the lions, whether to be exalted to the office of prime minister — to Daniel the reproach or the honor were alike before God.

"Now when Daniel knew that the writing was signed, he went into his house; and his windows being open in his chamber toward Jerusalem, he kneeled upon his knees three times a day, and prayed, and gave thanks before his God, as he did aforetime." The strength of the man, his refuge and his comfort, are found in prayer. A prayerless man is a graceless man. The disciples, as they watched the Lord, came to the conclusion that there was some vital inter-relatedness, inter-connectedness between his outward life of power and miracles, and his inward, private life of prayer and intercession. They came to the Lord and said, "Lord, teach us to pray" (Luke 11:1). Robert Murry M'Cheynne once said, "When a man is down on his knees and alone before God, that he is and nothing more." The outward life of Daniel was beautiful and noble in the court before the Babylonians, because his inward life was wholly devout and pure.

A Place of Prayer

Daniel had a place of prayer. Most Jewish houses had flat roofs. Apparently, on the flat roof of the home of this prime minister, he had a little chapel. And the windows of it opened toward Jerusalem. He had a place of prayer. The women in Philippi had a place of prayer, down on the riverside. It was in that place of prayer, down by the riverside, that Lydia, the Thyratiran businesswoman, came to know the Lord, the first convert to Christ in Paul's European journey (Acts 16:14, 15).

One of the most memorable things ever to happen to me

concerns a place of prayer. As a teenager, I was holding a meeting in Central West Texas. A rancher there invited me to a noon meal. After the meal he invited me to walk and to visit with him. The ranch house was built at the bottom of a mesa. We ascended to the top of the mesa and came to a clump of small trees. Their heads were bent inward to make a little covered area on the inside. In the center of that covered area, there was a root that came up and over and back down into the ground. When we stood there he said: "This is my place of prayer. I come here every day. I kneel and put both of my hands on that root, and I talk to God." He continued, "Today, I wanted you to kneel here by my side and let me pray for you." So he knelt down with both his hands on that root. He asked me to kneel down by his side, and when I did so, he prayed for me. At the time I had no idea why he should ask God to help me in those areas of life he mentioned in his intercession, but in the unfolding days and years, I have come to see God's answers to his prayers in those very areas he so earnestly laid before the Lord's throne of grace.

A Time of Prayer

I have a prayer rug by my bed, a beautiful prayer rug that I got in Teheran. Every day, on that prayer rug by the side of my bed, I pray. David had a place to pray, and a time to pray. He kneeled down and prayed three times a day. At the blush of the dawn in the morning; at the brightness of high noon; and in the shadows and twilight of the night, the sweet psalmist of Israel prayed. He wrote, "As for me, I will call upon God; and the Lord shall save me. Evening, and morning, and at noon, will I pray, and cry aloud: and he shall hear my voice" (Ps. 55:16, 17). Three times a day: in the morning, at noon, and in the evening, did Daniel pray.

A Posture of Prayer

And there was a posture in Daniel's praying. He kneeled down upon his knees and prayed in submission, in humility, in yielded surrender. He bowed before the Lord and prayed. I do not deny that you can pray, lying prostrate in bed. You can pray when you walk or drive the car. You can pray while at work, sitting down, or standing up. But kneeling in prayer does something psychologically to the soul.

The Kneeling Camel

The camel at the close of day
Kneels down upon the sandy plain
To have his burden lifted off
And rest to gain.

My soul, thou too shouldst to thy knees
When daylight draweth to a close,
And let thy master lift thy load,
And grant repose.

Else how canst thou tomorrow meet,
With all tomorrow's work to do,
If thou thy burden all the night
Dost carry through?

The camel kneels at break of day
To have his guide replace the load,
Then rises up anew to take
The desert road.

So thou shouldst kneel at morning dawn,
That God may give thee daily care;
Assured that He no load too great
Will make thee bear.

— *Anna Temple*

If I knew how to do it, all of us would pray in this sanctuary down on our knees, as our staff and as our deacons do. All through the Word of the Lord, His people knelt and prayed. When Solomon dedicated the temple, he kneeled down upon his knees before all the congregation of Israel, and spread forth his hands toward heaven, and said, "Lord God of Israel." When the blessed Jesus in Gethsemane prayed He kneeled down on His knees. When Stephen, Christ's first martyr, was beaten to the earth by stones, he cried with a loud voice, down on his knees, "Lord Jesus, receive my spirit" (Acts 7:59, 60). When the Apostle Paul spoke at Miletus with the elders from Ephesus, he prayed with them all, down on his knees (Acts 20:36). And Daniel kneeled down three times a day, and prayed, and gave thanks to God as before.

What did this man have to be thankful for? He had been hounded and badgered and lied about and persecuted, yet he kneeled down, and gave thanks to God, as before. That is when the Christian shines. I suppose anyone could be thankful for blessings whether they believed in God or not. Even Nikita Khrushchev once referred to being "thankful to God" for so and so. Yet he is an atheist, a Communist. I suppose anyone could be buoyant, joyous, happy and grateful when everything is shining and going his way. But to thank God in adversity, and to believe that all things work together for good to them that love the Lord, to give thanks, this is the test of a godly man. "Lord, you have been good to me, even in sorrow and trial."

Looking Toward God

Daniel prayed with his windows open toward Jerusalem, the lattices flung apart toward the holy city and the holy sanctuary. The city was dear to his heart, even though it lay in ruins. For seventy years silence had descended upon God's holy house. But it was precious to Daniel, for in that place the glory of God had been seen, and in that place the voice of God's love had been heard.

In faith he opened his windows toward the sanctuary of the Lord. He believed the promise of God that the people would return, that the city would be rebuilt, and that the temple should rise again.

Daniel could have opened his windows upon the market place. Or he could have opened his windows upon the throng passing by. He could have opened his windows and looked upon those sparkling domes of the politicians who were then contriving his own destruction in Babylon. But when time came to pray, Daniel opened his windows toward Jerusalem and the sanctuary of God.

Let me read to you from II Chronicles 6, at the dedication of the temple: "Solomon . . . kneeled down upon his knees before all the congregation of Israel, and spread forth his hands toward heaven, And said . . . If they sin against thee, (for there is no man which sinneth not,) and thou be angry with them, and deliver them over before their enemies, and they carry them away captives unto a land far off or near; . . . If they return to thee with all their heart and with all their soul in the land of their captivity, . . . and pray toward their land, . . . and toward the city which thou has chosen, and toward the house which I have built for thy name: Then hear thou from the heavens . . . and forgive thy people which have sinned against thee. . . . bring them again unto the land which thou gavest to them and to their fathers" (II Chron. 6:13, 14, 36, 38, 39, 25). That is what Daniel was doing. He was opening windows toward Jerusalem and the sanctuary, and praying to the Lord who answers prayer in behalf of His people.

LIGHT FROM HEAVEN

I can just imagine the light that streamed back from those windows out of heaven to the great statesman. I am not talking about just judgment or discernment or discrimination in political life. God, indeed, had made him a mighty and wise leader and statesman. But I am not speaking about just political life and judgment. I am talking about the vision glorious. Do you remember when the Lord Jesus said to the Jewish people of His day, "Your father Abraham rejoiced to see my day: and he saw it, and was glad" (John 8:56)? I think Daniel did the same thing. He turned his face toward Jerusalem and toward the sanctuary, which was the only type of Christ he had in that dispensation. And when the Lord streamed back visions to his heart (we will come to this in time in the ninth chapter of the book of Daniel) the prophet statesman used language that is identical to that of the Apostle Paul. As Daniel prayed, God opened his heart and showed him the things of Christ. It was as though Daniel were standing at the cross himself. It was as though he were there at the empty tomb himself. It was as though he saw the ascension and the coming of Christ in glory. God answered with light streaming from the portals of heaven. The only type of Christ Daniel had was the Temple, with its seven-branch lampstand, the golden altar of incense, and the mercy seat on the Ark of the Covenant. In reverential faithfulness, he turned his face in supplication toward them.

Daniel had only the type. But today we have the reality. Our hearts are opened toward the heavenly Jerusalem, and we have the reality of the light of forgiveness in our great Mediator, Jesus Christ. For we have not come to Mt. Sinai, with its thunder and lightning, and its great earthquakes whereby even Moses said, "I exceedingly fear and quake. But ye are come unto mount Sion, and unto the city of the living God, the heavenly Jerusalem, and to an innumerable company of angels, To the general assembly and church of the firstborn, which are written in heaven, and to God the Judge of all, and to the spirits of just men made perfect, And to Jesus the mediator of the new covenant, and to the blood of sprinkling, that speaketh better things than that of Abel" (Heb. 12:21-24). Our windows are open now to the new Jerusalem, and to the Savior who is typified by the lampstand, and the altar and the mercy seat.

Light From Home

"Now when Daniel knew that the writing was signed, he went into his house; and his windows being open in his chamber toward Jerusalem, he kneeled upon his knees three times a day, and prayed, and gave thanks before his God, as he did aforetime." Where did Daniel learn to do that? How did he come to practice that? I will tell you where. Daniel was an old man now, about ninety years of age. He had been taken captive out of Judah when he was but a boy. But back in that land where his fathers were buried, in that land from whence he came as a captive and a slave, there had been a mother and a father and a godly home. They had taught their little boy the name of God and the worship of the true Jehovah. Throughout the years of his life, Daniel had remembered the teaching of those godly parents. All the dazzling glitter of Babylon could not blot the memory out of his heart. Now an old man, ninety years of age, facing the greatest trial of his life, death by being torn apart by lions, Daniel turns his face toward the memory of mother and father and home. He never forgot them. Nor do we. Nor will our children if they are brought up in the love and admonition of the Lord.

"When Daniel knew the writing was signed, he went into his house; and his windows being open in his chamber toward Jerusalem, he kneeled upon his knees three times a day, and prayed, and gave thanks before his God, as he did aforetime." God make us like that! Do it for us, Lord! Do it now! Give us that same openness, unashamedness, and commitment to the Lord Jesus. Here I am, Lord. The windows of my heart and life are open toward Thee. I come, Lord, with my wife, and my children, and we kneel down on our knees and pray before Thee. Oh, I am coming, Lord. I give my heart to Thee. I take Jesus as the Savior and Sovereign of my life. Do it now. Do it now. God will bless you and angels attend you, as you come like Daniel to kneel before the Lord.

THE LESSON OF DANIEL

A proud king reigned in Babylon the great;
A pure youth dreamed, to goodness consecrate.
The youth turned eyes to Heaven, with a prayer;
The king appraised his wealth and kingdom fair.
But God disdained the kingdom — it was gone;
The humble youth prayed earnestly at dawn.
No lions' den nor furnace breathing fire
Can frighten him whom Godly thoughts inspire.
The tyrant's taunts are as the winter grim
Whose insults pass as God's bright spring comes in.
The hosts of error, clad in stern array,
Inflame the world, then glumly fade away.
Proud kings and mighty kingdoms suffer loss;
Love lives! — through Godly visions and a Cross.

— Thomas Curtis Clark

From *The Old Testament and the Fine Arts* edited by Cynthia Pearl Maus, p. 716. Copyright, 1954, by Harper & Brothers. New York.

CHAPTER 10

ANGELS AND LIONS

ANGELS AND LIONS

Then the king commanded, and they brought Daniel, and cast him into the den of lions. Now the king spake and said unto Daniel, Thy God whom thou servest continually, he will deliver thee.

And a stone was brought, and laid upon the mouth of the den; and the king sealed it with his own signet, and with the signet of his lords; that the purpose might not be changed concerning Daniel.

Then the king went to his palace, and passed the night fasting: neither were instruments of musick brought before him: and his sleep went from him.

Then the king arose very early in the morning, and went in haste unto the den of lions.

And when he came to the den, he cried with a lamentable voice unto Daniel: and the king spake and said to Daniel, O Daniel, servant of the living God, is thy God, whom thou servest continually, able to deliver thee from the lions?

Then said Daniel unto the king, O king, live for ever.

My God hath sent his angel, and hath shut the lions' mouths, that they have not hurt me: forasmuch as before him innocency was found in me; and also before thee, O king, have I done no hurt.

Then was the king exceeding glad for him, and commanded that they should take Daniel up out of the den. So Daniel was taken up out of the den, and no manner of hurt was found upon him, because he believed in his God.

> And the king commanded, and they brought those men which had accused Daniel, and they cast them into the den of lions, them, their children, and their wives; and the lions had the mastery of them, and brake all their bones in pieces or ever they came at the bottom of the den.
>
> Daniel 6:16-24

The discussion today is an exposition of Daniel 6:11-23.

Deceived Darius

First of all, we look at the deceived Darius, who found himself in a den of his own making, a den of dilemma and agonizing frustration. He had signed and sealed a decree that, for thirty days, no one in his kingdom could pray or make appeal to any god except to him. The signed decree further stated that if anyone was found who violated that law, he was to be cast into a den of lions. So "this Daniel" was found, doing "as he did aforetime," praying to the true Jehovah, Lord of heaven. Verse 11 begins with that open, unashamed commitment of Daniel to his God.

Conspirators and informers were everywhere. They easily found Daniel down on his knees praying and making supplication before God. Then they came and spoke before the king concerning the king's decree. They said: "Didn't you sign a decree stating that any man that should ask anything of God or man for thirty days, save of thee, O king, shall be cast into the den of lions?" The king had to answer: "Yes, yes. The thing is true according to the law of the Medes and Persians which altereth not." Then they drove home their diabolical scheme. They said to the king, "That Daniel, which is of the children of the captivity of Judah, regardeth not thee, O king, nor the decree that thou hast signed, but maketh his petition three times a day" (Dan. 6:13).

Then the king, when he heard these words, was "sore displeased with himself." What a change! The day before he had attained the giddiest heights of ambition. He was declared a god. He was deified before the Persians and the Babylonians. But now he is a dupe. His courtiers have made a fool of him. They have made him look ridiculous. Is not that a portrayal of our humanity? From god down to dupe in one day! We can so quickly fall into a trap set for us by our arch enemy and adversary, the devil. This is but one more illustration of our awesome and total apostasy. We are a fallen people, all of us. Our minds, our hearts, our thoughts, our visions, our dreams, our ambitions, everything about us is fallen. We are apostate and lost. If such a postulate were presented in a book, we might argue against it with vehemence, but our problem lies in the bitterness of our own experience. There is no one who cannot find things in his or her life of which he or she is grossly ashamed.

There is no more dramatic story in the Bible than the story of the Lord God sending Elisha to Hazael to anoint him king over Syria. After speaking with Hazael, Elisha the prophet looked searchingly at him. And as he looked at him the prophet began to weep. Hazael asked Elisha, "Why weepeth my lord?" And Elisha replied, "Because I know the evil that thou wilt do unto the children of Israel." Then the prophet agonizingly described it. After the description Hazael answered Elisha and said, "But what, is thy servant a dog, that he should do this great thing?" (II Kings 8: 12, 13) But he did it. And all of us do. There is no one of us but who finds himself entrapped. We are duped, fallen, apostatized, depraved. All of us are sinners, lost. All of us. So likewise was this Darius, at heart one of the finest noblemen among monarchs, but caught by those who sought to snare his feet. Thus he found himself in the pit, in the den, agonizingly, frustratingly so.

"Then the king, when he heard these words, was sore displeased with himself, and he set his heart on Daniel to deliver him: and he labored till the going down of the sun to deliver him" (Dan. 6:14). But his princes and the enemies of Daniel were constitutional lawyers. They were skillful. They knew that law to the letter. The Book says that the "letter of the law killeth." It is the spirit that makes alive. And all through our courts of justice you will find shrewd lawyers driving home the letter, and violating the intent and spirit of the constitutional writers who sought to deliver us from such mechanisms. These men were shrewd and constitutional. They were unassailable. When the king tried to deliver Daniel they were not to be moved. "Know, O king, that the law of the Medes and Persians is, That no decree nor statute which the king establisheth may be changed" (Dan. 6:15). Here it is, written, signed, and sealed.

Stubborn Pride

Why should the kingdom of the Medes and the Persians have considered such stupidity as a law like this which could never be changed? Maybe it was because the people thought it would give a monarch pause before he made a decree. If a king realized his word could not be changed he would not be hasty in giving it. Certainly it could have been a blessing to the people in that it delivered them from constant change. They could count on and live by what was done. But there is also a facet in this story of Darius that is so true of a man. I refer to that questionable, debatable pride that makes him carry through a wrong action, just because he has sworn it or taken an oath to do it.

You have an identical instance of this pride in Herod Antipas. When Salome danced before the king, he was enamored with her. He was so delighted and pleased that he said, "I'll give you anything to the half of my kingdom." Herodias, her wicked mother, said, "Ask for the head of John the Baptist." When Herod heard that request he was grieved.

But for his oath's sake, and for the men who were around him, he gave commandment and the executioner chopped off the head of the Baptist (Mark 6:26, 27).

Until recent days, no officer in the army and no nobleman could live with himself, if he refused to accept the challenge to a duel. Alexander Hamilton, one of the most brilliant men of America, was the first secretary of the treasury under George Washington. He was the man who, through his federalist papers, helped to create the constitutional government of America. Yet he was killed in a duel by the unspeakable Aaron Burr. Is not that a strange thing? That streak of pride lies in all men. They will do wrong rather than lose face. Whole nations are like that. They go to war, go to any extremity, rather than lose face. So Darius, as the lawyers stood before him and drove home their constitutional point, did wrong rather than lose face.

But he was displeased with himself, so much so that he set his heart to deliver Daniel. But his efforts availed nothing. Finally, at the end of the day, the king commanded, and they brought Daniel and cast him into the den, and the king sealed it with his own signet. But the king did one other thing, God bless him. "Now the king spake and said unto Daniel, Thy God whom thou servest continually, he will deliver thee" (Dan. 6:16). Is not that something? This heathen monarch has turned preacher, comforter and exhorter. "Daniel, Thy God whom thou servest continually, he will deliver thee." And, is not it great to see a heathen king stand on tiptoe to see the dawn of the Gospel? "Thy God will deliver thee." His heart is in every syllable. "Thy God, personal Lord, whom thou servest continually, he will deliver thee." What an impact, what an impression did Daniel make upon that heathen king! He was thoroughly persuaded that the Lord God of Daniel could not but deliver so faithful, so noble and so steadfast a servant.

The Delivered Daniel

So they took Daniel and they delivered him to the dungeon. This is exactly as the shrewd, clandestine courtiers thought it would come to pass. Exactly. Daniel refused to change his habits of worship. He refused to change his praying to God. Refusing to close his windows opened toward Jerusalem, he bravely disobeyed the decree that would separate him from the Lord God in heaven. I can just see the old man. He is nearly ninety years of age now. His hair is white. With dignity and calm self-assurance, he walks into the den and the dungeon. The man who fears God only, need fear no one else. So Daniel walked into the den with quiet trust in the Lord.

What happened? There was another deliverance. The Lord God sent an angel and shut the lions mouths, and Daniel spent the night in quiet rest. Why, Daniel was more at rest in the den of lions than Darius was in the palace with all its comforts and luxuries. Is not the night for rest? In the day we work; at night we rest. In the day we are abroad, at night we are home. In the day God fills the earth with light and with stimulated activity. But in the night God hushes the sound, He stops the song of the birds, and He draws the curtains of tenderest darkness, and says, "hush." Psalm 127 avows, "He giveth his beloved sleep."

The Lord God not only sent an angel to watch over Daniel, but He also whispered a commandment into the ears of those savage, ravenous, and carnivorous beasts. He said: "One of my servants is coming down to spend the night with you. Receive him cordially and hospitably. Make him comfortable. Hurt not a hair of his head. Lay down your shaggy mane that he may use it for a pillow." At the end of this chapter, these lions ravenously destroyed the enemies of Daniel. But Daniel they watch over, and care for, and guard, and keep. The angels and the lions. "Angels and Lions." I can just see Daniel as he lays his head upon the shaggy mane of one of those giant kings of the forest. The saintly prophet softly sings a lullaby as he goes to sleep: "Angels and lions watching over me. Angels and lions watching over me." And God's servant is asleep.

Here I cannot help but think of Simon Peter, in Acts 12. Herod Agrippa had cut off the head of James, the brother of John. When he saw that the murder pleased the leaders in Jerusalem, he arrested Peter also, and put him in the prison to keep him for execution the next day. Then follows the story of the angel coming down and casting off the manacles and chains that incarcerated Peter. The great iron door of the dark prison opened by itself and let him out into the street and set him free. When the angel came down to deliver Peter, what was Peter doing? Do you remember? He was sound asleep, chained between those two guards! Sound asleep he was, and so sound asleep that the Book tells us the angel came and smote him on the side and said: "Wake up, Simon Peter! Don't you know you're supposed to have your head cut off in the morning? Wake up!" "Angels and lions, watching over me." And Daniel fell asleep in the confidence of the shepherdly care of his Lord. "My God hath sent his angel, and hath shut the lions' mouths."

OUR DEN OF LIONS

The experience of Daniel is a type and a figure of all of our lives. We are all in some den of lions. I am not speaking of stuffed animals that have the name and not the nature. The trials of a Christian are not sentimental. They are real. The Christian way is never always silken, smooth, and soft. It is sometimes hard and rigorous. We ought never to speak to youngsters and young people as though the Christian life were nothing but a primrose path and a bed of roses. It is sometimes difficult. The writing has been signed against us.

The progress of the Christian is through antagonism, trial, and temptation.

> Am I a soldier of the cross?
>   A follower of the Lamb?
> And shall I fear to own His cause
>   Or blush to speak His name?
>
> Must I be carried to the skies
>   On flowry beds of ease,
> While others fought to win the prize
>   And sailed thru bloody seas?
>
> Since I must fight if I would reign —
>   Increase my courage, Lord!
> I'll bear the toil, endure the pain,
>   Supported by Thy Word.

That is the Christian way. All of us find ourselves in some den of lions. Here in the book of Daniel, in the first chapter, Daniel was battling with drink. In the second chapter he was to be liquidated. In the third and fourth chapters, he took his life in his hands, delivering God's message to the king, speaking bluntly and truthfully. In the third chapter his friends have been thrown into the fiery furnace. Here he is in a dungeon of lions. That is the Christian faith. If Abraham is called to go out, he moves, not knowing whither he goes. He takes his whole family with him, not knowing where he is going. When Moses is called, he finds his pilgrimage through a wilderness. When Elijah stands before Jezebel and Ahab, he is threatened with death. The Apostle Paul wrote, "Yea, and all that will live godly in Christ Jesus shall suffer persecution" (II Tim. 3:12). The Lord's brother, James, starts his epistle with words of encouragement for Christians who fall into heavy trial. It is for all of us. We all face the lions. We are all in some den.

Those without God in the world also face trial and trouble

and lions. But there is a difference between them and us. It is found in the possession of the presence of God. God makes the difference. Go behind the Christian's back to stab him, and God is behind his back. Go in front of a Christian to cut him down, and God is in front of him. Waylay him on the side of the road, and God is on his right hand, and on his left hand. As Paul said in Acts 27 of the awesome storm that wrecked his ship, "For there stood by me this night the angel of God" (verse 23). Paul in the Mamertine Dungeon, in the fourth chapter of his last letter, the second letter to Timothy, said: "No man stood with me, but all men forsook me. . . . Notwithstanding the Lord stood with me, and strengthened me . . . and I was delivered out of the mouth of the lion" (II Tim. 4:16, 17). It is God who makes the difference.

WE CANNOT LOSE

When we read this story of Daniel, the question cannot but come to our minds: "What if the lions had eaten him up? What if they had broken his bones and shredded his body? What if the lions had devoured him?" The answer is still the same, he still would have won. He could not lose. He still would have triumphed. It could have been God's will that he die, as it could have been God's will that he be delivered. The important thing is not the deliverance. The important thing is God's will. God did not deliver John the Baptist. They cut off his head and he lay in a pool of his own blood. It was not God's will that Jesus be delivered. They nailed Him to the cross. It was not God's will that James, the brother of John, be delivered. Herod Agrippa cut off his head. It was not God's will for Stephen to be delivered. They beat out his life with stones as they crushed him into the dust. It was not God's will that Paul be ultimately delivered. The executioner on the Ostian Road outside Rome cut off his head. Because he was a Roman citizen, Paul could not be crucified. But a vast throng of other Christians were crucified. When you go to the great Coliseum in Rome and look down, remember in that place there were thousands of Christians who were fed to the lions. Sometimes it is not God's will that the Christian be delivered. But it is God's will that we should have a triumphant victory. *Via Crucis, via lucis.* "The way of the cross is the way of life."

The Christian is never defeated. For him down is up and black is bright and light and glory. "Well," you say, "John the Baptist had his head severed. Is not that a disaster?" No! It was his introduction and his presentation in glory. He went to heaven just like that, with the swift stroke of an ax. Why, you might as well speak of a man who spites a ship by casting it into the waters. He does not destroy it. He just launches it. The ship, though it is made on the land, is built for the sea. And the child of God is not at home until he is in heaven.

> I am a stranger here
> Heaven is my home.
> Earth is a desert drear,
> Heaven is my home.
> Sorrows and dangers stand
> Round me on every hand,
> Heaven is my fatherland,
> Heaven is my home.

Had Daniel lost his life, the angels would have carried his soul to Abraham's bosom. Does not the Book say so? If it is God's will for us to live, we are delivered, as the three Hebrew children and as Daniel were delivered. But if it is not God's will, we are caught up to be with the Lord in glory, as Stephen, and as Antipas, an unknown martyr in Pergamos in the second chapter of the Revelation, were caught up. Whether it be to live under the guarding, shepherdly, loving care of God, or whether it is to die, the angels watch over us to bear us on snowy wings to glory.

> Oh, come angel band.
> Come and around me stand.
> Oh, bear me away on your snowy wings,
> To my immortal home,
> Bear me away on your snowy wings,
> To my immortal home.

"Angels and lions watching over me." We are hid with Christ in God. We are kept forever by His omnipotent hand. Doing His will and seeking His Holy purpose for us in the earth, we will rejoice in God's best choice for us, whether it be to live or to die.

Will you let God give you His best today? His most precious deliverance for us is found in our Lord Jesus. Through Him God can deliver you from sin and guilt and death. Let God deliver you, as He did Daniel. Open your heart and let it be filled with assurance for life and for death. Do it today. Do it now. Sing that lullaby of the soul with Daniel, "Angels and lions watching over me."

DANIEL

> Daniel was a godly man
> And thankful through his days . . .
> He never failed to pray to God
> And give Him all the praise.
>
> His trials were so many,
> And he was tempted sore . . .
> But he was saved by righteousness,
> And the godly cloak he wore.
>
> Interpreting the royal dreams
> Through wisdom from on high . . .
> He ever gave the praise to God,
> As his life did verify.

In the fiery furnace
    And in the lions' den . . .
The flames were stayed, the jaws were set
    Before oppressing men.

But he emerged triumphant,
    For God was ever near . . .
He guards His children from all harm
    When danger does appear.

Through our temptations and our trials,
    On life's tempestuous ways . . .
I thank Thee, God, for Daniel,
    And for his life of praise.

Upon my knees, I pray that God,
    Will make me thankful too . . .
And worthy of His love and care . . .
    I know He'll see me through!

                  — *Ruth Ricklefs*

From *The Old Testament and the Fine Arts* edited by Cynthia Pearl Maus, p. 713. Copyright, 1954, by Harper & Brothers. New York.

THE TRIAL AND THE TRIUMPH

CHAPTER 11

THE TRIAL AND THE TRIUMPH

> Then king Darius wrote unto all people, nations, and languages, that dwell in all the earth; Peace be multiplied unto you.
> I make a decree, That in every dominion of my kingdom men tremble and fear before the God of Daniel; for he is the living God, and steadfast for ever, and his kingdom that which shall not be destroyed, and his dominion shall be even unto the end.
> He delivereth and rescueth, and he worketh signs and wonders in heaven and in earth, who hath delivered Daniel from the power of the lions.
> So this Daniel prospered in the reign of Darius, and in the reign of Cyrus the Persian.
>
> Daniel 6:25-28

Beginning at chapter 7 and going through chapter 12 in the book of Daniel, the subject matter is altogether different. The first six chapters of Daniel compose a narrative. But the last six chapters of the book concern the visions and the prophecies that God gave to this Babylonian captive. The book of Daniel is divided into two separate and distinct parts, just as is the book of the Revelation. Revelation 1 through 11 are one thing. Chapters 12 through 22 are something else. Both books, Daniel and Revelation, are divided exactly in the middle.

The narrative of the life of Daniel closes with these words:

"So this Daniel prospered in the reign of Darius, and in the reign of Cyrus the Persian" (6:28). This means that Daniel, born around 620 B.C., lived to about 535 B.C. His life covered the entire Babylonian captivity.

We shall look upon Daniel as a type of the trials and triumphs of the Christian, a type of the people of God. The Apostle Paul wrote in I Corinthians 10:11, "Now all these things happened unto them for ensamples: and they are written for our admonition, upon whom the ends of the world are come." What I read, therefore, in the Book of Daniel concerning the life of this prophet-statesman, I am to accept in God's Holy Word as an encouragement for my own life. We shall, therefore, look upon Daniel as a type of all of God's people who travel through the wilderness of this world. There are three trials Daniel sustained which are common to us: First, the trial of the flesh; second, the trial of the mind and the intellect; and third, the trial of the soul, which is a religious, spiritual trial.

The Trial of the Flesh

Let us speak first of the trial of the flesh. This is the trial of which we read in Daniel 1. The temptation to the young man was fierce. He was a captive in a foreign court. He had been deported into a strange country. But in that strange land and as a captive slave in that court, he was given unusual, preferential treatment. He himself was of the seed royal. Because Daniel was fair of countenance and agile of mind, the great golden king, Nebuchadnezzar, had chosen him to be trained, educated, taught in all of the wisdom of the Chaldeans. He was to be one of the wise men, one of the Magi. As a trained counselor he was to stand before the king.

The place of Daniel was one of tremendous opportunity. His life belonged to royalty itself. There were uncounted numbers of subjects of the king, citizens of Babylon and Babylonia, who did not live in the king's court, who did not eat at the king's table, who did not drink the king's wine, and who did not share the luxuries and comforts of the king's palace. But this Judean captive had opportunity to enjoy them all. Though he was uprooted from his country and made a slave in the court of Babylon, he had every open door for promotion and advancement.

Therein came the most intimate of all of the trials and temptations that can come to a child of God. For the temptation is to be gracious, to be appreciative, to be friendly, to be nice, to be socially acceptable, to be neighborly, at the price of principle. You could not imagine a situation in which any man could ever find himself, that would have in it so many facets of what it is to be pleasing to the world and traitorous toward God. Daniel was not tempted to become a thug or a murderer or a malefactor. His temptation was to be nice, to be congenial, to be socially acceptable. It was the way of advancement and promotion. There was spread before him the king's table. Eat. There was spread before him the king's liquor. Drink. His advancement depended upon his gracious response.

When Daniel spoke to the captain, to the master of the king's household, the master explained to him that this was the program of the king himself. The bounties of the monarch, the largesse of the kingdom, the hospitality and the graciousness and the kindness of the king himself, were all bound up in this sharing of the king's table and of the king's liquors. I submit to you, that in my judgment there could never have come a trial or temptation as fierce as that or as intimate. What should the young man do? Remember, he was a youth, doubtless in his later teens. He was away from home, family, and country; he was away from his people. He was all by himself, a youth in the king's court. These luxuries at the king's table were offered him in anticipation of his choice as a kingdom counselor.

The decision he made, he made for himself, which reminds me to say emphatically, that what a young person is, he decides for himself. I do not consort with these materialistic sociologists and other pseudo-scientists who, when they see a youth in trouble (he is breaking God's law, he is breaking man's law, he is breaking society's law), say: "It is not his fault. He is a victim of his environment. He is a victim of society. He is a victim of circumstance. He is a victim of his friends." No! That is a lie of the first order. When any youth, anywhere, decides something, he decides for himself, and he is responsible for what he decides.

God made us all alike. We are sensitive to right and wrong. Whether we are young black people in Uganda in the heart of deepest Africa, or whether we are teenagers in any high school, we all are accountable for our decisions in life. We all are sensitive to right and wrong. When we choose wrong we know it. Daniel was a teenager when he faced the choice and he made it knowing full well the attendant alternatives. Youth is responsible. Youth chooses. God made us that way. That is what it is to be free, namely to be free to choose, to be morally accountable. That is what it is to be created in the image of God — we decide for ourselves. Look at this poem. The unknown poet writes exactly of that moral freedom by which God created us all.

> When in the dim beginning of the years
> God mixed in man the rapture and the tears,
> And scattered through his brain the starry stuff,
> God said: "Behold, yet this is not enough;
> For I must test his spirit and make sure
> That he can bear the vision and endure.
>
> "I will leave man to make the fateful guess,
> Will leave him torn between the 'no' and the 'yes.'
> Leave him unresting 'till he rests in me,

Drawn upward by the choice that makes him free;
Leave him in tragic loneliness to choose
With all in life to win, or all to lose."

God made us that way. We are absolutely, morally free.
They may put our bodies in prison, but our souls remain
free. They may impound and incarcerate our physical
frames behind stone walls and iron bars, but our spirits are
free.

What you are is a concomitant and a summation of the
choices you make in your life. When you choose the weak
and the lower, you become weaker and weaker. But when
you choose the strong and the higher, you become stronger
and stronger. You are what you decide. You are responsible
and what you do is not the fault of someone else.

Yet we tend to blame others for our sins. That is a trait
which has been in us from the beginning. When God stood
before Adam, Adam said, "The woman, she did it." When
God stood before the woman, the woman said, "The serpent, he did it." Always it is someone else. But in God's
sight, we are personally, individually accountable. There are
some who sell their souls for a mess of pottage. They will
compromise for any advancement or preferment. But there
are some who will be true to God unto death. I do not know
of a nobler commitment to God's call in human story than
that of John Bunyan. He spent twelve years languishing in
prison, in Bedford jail. Any day of those twelve years he
could have had his freedom if he would have agreed to say
one sentence, "I will not preach the Gospel any more." That
is all he had to say, "I will not preach the Gospel any more."
But when John Bunyan was confronted with that decision
he said, "I would rather stay here in prison until the moss
grows on my eyelids, than promise not to preach the Gospel of the grace of the Son of God."

That is the temptation of the flesh, the trial of the flesh, namely, the temptation to compromise spiritual principles for personal gain. We all face it. We all experience it.

The Trial of the Mind

The second trial is that of the mind, the intellect. This trial is found in Daniel 2. The dilemma of the dream recorded in Daniel 2 is succinctly stated. It was simply placed before the Magi of Babylon, "You tell me what that dream was, and its meaning, or you are dead." That is plain. Anyone can understand that, can they not? The king said: "You give me the answer or you are liquidated. Either tell me or you die. Either answer (and I will know if the answer is correct or not, because I had the dream) or you will be executed, one or the other." That is very plain, is it not? What a trial of the mind, of the intellect! Nebuchadnezzar said, "You either tell me or you die."

The Magi, the astrologers, the magicians, the sorcerers, all of that motley throng in the court of the king, were there to give answers. That is why they were chosen. That is what they were trained for, to give the answers. "We know," they said. "We know. We are the knowing ones. We are the Magi. We are the wisemen. We are the Gnostics. We know." That is what they said, and that is why they were there, to answer. But when the king laid before them this simple dilemma, "You either tell me this dream or you are dead," they said: "O king, the gods that be in heaven have given thee a kingdom and thou art a golden monarch, but thou hast asked an hard thing. There is no man in the earth who can answer a question like that. None. He does not live. That answer lies with the gods alone. We are forced to face it. We do not know." This is the trial of the mind, of the intellect.

Our world is overwhelmed and thronged by these modern Gnostics, these all-wise knowing ones. They have all of the answers. They say: "We are the students and scholars of the age. We teach in the universities and colleges. We write books. We have all of the answers, and we tell you certainly the Bible is not true. We tell you with assurance there is no God." They write these negations down in polysyllabic nomenclature in learned books. The learned avow: "There is no such thing as the Spirit of Jesus guiding the destiny of this world. We know." Since they purport to be the all-knowing ones, we bring to them the simplest questions: "Where did I come from? Where am I going? What is the purpose and the meaning of life? Where did everything find its origin and what is its meaning?" And these modern Magi, these all-knowing ones, look at us in blank stupidity and say, "We have no idea!" That is why modern, existentialist philosophy is one of abject despair. It is a teaching of blackness and darkness. They say: "There is not any purpose and there is not any reason behind the universe. There is not any divine will. This whole universe, and we in it, are nothing but adventitiously placed blobs of matter in some kind of a swirling, atomic mass that has no meaning. It came from nowhere, it is going nowhere, and it has no purpose behind it." No wonder they are despairing. Yet that is the answer of the Magi today, "We do not know."

Why do they not know? The answer is very plain. This is the trial of the mind, the trial of the intellect. There is no one who can reveal the secrets of the meaning of the universe and of life but Almighty God. All that man can do is observe. He just looks. The sun apparently rises in the east and sets in the west. Man just looks at it. The flower blooms and bears fruit. Man just looks at it. Life grows and multiplies. Man just looks at it. Here is mitosis. He just looks at it. Here is osmosis. He just looks at it. Here is gravity. He just looks at it. Here are all of these great laws of the universe. Man just looks at them. He is not able to explain any of these things. He does not know because the answer lies in God.

The only way we ever know the real meaning of life is in the self-revelation and self-disclosure of Almighty God. A man can study forever, and never really know. We never know until God discloses the truth and the meaning. It is God who reveals secrets.

What did Daniel do when he was faced with that dilemma of the dream? He took it to God, and then having an answer, he came before the king and said: "There is a God in heaven who reveals secrets. He discloses." At the conclusion of the amazing revelation, the king answered Daniel and said, "Of a truth it is, that your God is a God of gods, and a Lord of kings, and a revealer of secrets." The only answer you will ever find to the simplest questions you want to ask (questions about yourself, the world, the universe, the future and the past in which you are inextricably bound) lies in the Lord God. That is why the Apostle Paul wrote in the first Corinthian letter: "The foolishness of God is wiser than men; and the weakness of God is stronger than men. God hath chosen the foolish things of the world to confound the wise; and God hath chosen the weak things of the world to confound the things which are mighty; And base things of the world, and things which are despised, hath God chosen, yea, and things which are not, to bring to nought things that are: That no flesh should glory in his presence" (I Cor. 1:25, 27, 28, 29). The apostle adds in the second chapter of the first Corinthian letter, "But the natural man receiveth not the things of the Spirit of God: for they are foolishness unto him: neither can he know them, because they are spiritually discerned" (I Cor. 2:14).

A man has a spiritual faculty inside of him. He has a natural mind that can reason and he has natural eyes that can observe. But a man has another faculty, an intuitive faculty, a spiritual faculty. It is with the eyes of this intuitive, spiritual faculty that a man sees God. We endure as seeing Him who is invisible. By Him we understand the things of the universe, where they come from, even as the author of Hebrews wrote in Hebrews 11:3, "Through faith we understand that the worlds were framed by the word of God, so that things which are seen were not made of things which do appear." In the wisdom of God we learn what life means, and of the great consummation and goal toward which it is reaching. Without God we will never understand. This is the trial of the mind, namely, to find answers apart from God.

THE TRIAL OF THE SOUL

The third trial is one of the soul, of the spirit. It is a religious trial. It is found in Daniel 6.

Three times, once in the ninth chapter and twice in the tenth chapter, Daniel is called "the beloved:" "O Daniel, a man greatly beloved" (10:11). Daniel was loved in heaven by the Lord, by the angels, and by the saints. He was greatly loved. Why was he not greatly loved in earth? In the sixth chapter of Daniel we are astonished to discover that he was hated by many of his peers. Daniel was a man with a genius for statesmanship to guide the destinies of an empire. He was impeccable in his judgments and administration, against whom no one could impute error or mistake or wrong. And he was a benevolent, kind, gracious leader of his people. Wouldn't you think he would command universal approbation? Wouldn't it seem he would have been as loved in earth as he was in heaven? Yet this Daniel was detested for his goodness and for all of the righteousness in his soul. How do you explain that? This is the trial of the spirit. The first man in the Bible who laid down his life was a martyr to his religious faith. His name was Abel. And in the book of the Revelation, the last ones who will lay down their lives are martyrs to their religious faith. They will be slain for loving God.

The world of religion is sometimes a strange world as men dictate it. Did you ever hear of a like decree such as the king signed in the sixth chapter of the book of Daniel? "There shall be no supplication made to any god for thirty days." What an enormous extravagance! Who could afford it? If the sun sears the land, there is no supplication for rain. If pestilence decimates the people, there is no prayer for the staying of the plague. If fire or enemy comes to destroy the kingdom, there is no appeal for heavenly help. One might just as well make a decree that if a man is sick, he must not call the physician. If he is drowning, he must not appeal for one to throw out a life-line from the shore. If one is wrong, he is not to appeal for forgiveness.

Where did such an idea come from? The answer is simple. You see it every day in your own life. These men manipulated their own gods. They used their gods for selfish purposes. All of us are made in the image of our gods. We are continually made so. Their gods were gods who could be used and manipulated. The men made the decisions, not the gods. They set the time, not the gods. Their gods were to wait upon them. If they chose for that decree to last thirty days or ninety days, or one hundred and twenty days, or ten years, or a lifetime, it was up to them to decide. They set the date. They made the decisions. They set out and signed the decree. And their gods waited upon them.

Can you imagine the response of Daniel to that kind of a god? Can you imagine how he reacted to that kind of manipulation of a god who could be cajoled, a god who could be made to wait upon his wishes and desires? Can you imagine the response of the great prophet of the sovereign Jehovah, a God who reigned over all of the earth? The great God who has all of the world in His hands — manipulate *Him?* Do you think Daniel could look upon his God as though He waited upon human decrees, as though He were servant and slave? Can you imagine how Daniel felt? Oh, the great sovereign Jehovah Lord God in whose sight the nations are like a drop in the bucket, in whose presence the peoples of the earth are just like a fine, inconsequential dust in a balance! Ah, the great Lord God, in whose hands my life is bound, our lives are bound, our worlds exist, the guide and the sovereign of all time and history! Ah, I fall before Thee! I cannot understand how a man could come before Jehovah God and not bow, not seek His face, His favor, His will, and His purpose.

This was the trial of the soul which Daniel faced, and which we all face as God's people. Daniel faced it and was cast into the lions' den rather than fail to bow before the mighty sovereign of all the earth.

THE TRIUMPH

But now the triumph. When that lions' den was opened and Daniel came out alive and unharmed, the king wrote unto the peoples, nations, languages in the earth: "I make another decree. The whole world is to fear and tremble before the God of Daniel." Look how the king described the mighty, delivering God. He did not use polysyllabic descriptions such as "God the Omnipotent," or "God the Omniscent," or "God the Immutable," but he said, "the God of Daniel," the Lord incarnate in that man. A demonstration of God in faith and in life is your only witness that the world ever knows or observes. What a testimony when Daniel came out of that dungeon! I can just see the awe with which the king and his cabinet and his subjects looked upon him. Think of the encouragement to his Jewish people and think of the blessings to the name of God in the earth, that came in the triumph of Daniel, God's prophet-statesman. Daniel lives in heaven, he lives in this book, and he lives in our hearts forever. Lord, that we could shine and glow in our witness and testimony before Jesus like that! When the world looks at us, that they might praise the name of the great Lord God who reigns in glory!

The triumph of Daniel became a type of God's victory for His people in the earth. Daniel is a book of prophecy as the Revelation is a book of prophecy. Three times does it say in the Revelation, "the words of this prophecy." Daniel is called by Jesus, "the prophet." So the book is a prophecy. Daniel, therefore, is a type of things yet to come.

Daniel is a type of Christ. Daniel was placed in a tomb. He was as though he were dead. Over the door of that dungeon-den there was rolled a stone and it was sealed with the king's seal. Down there, fed to the lions, buried, he was as one dead, delivered to death. In this he was a type of Christ, crucified, placed in a sepulcher, a great stone rolled over it and sealed by the seal of the empire. But out of the sepulcher the Christ arose, as out of it Daniel came.

Daniel is a type of the remnant which will be saved out of the fierce, burning tribulation at the consummation of the age. He is a type of the salvation of the Jewish remnant in the seventh chapter of the book of the Revelation. In addition, Daniel is a type of those who are sealed and who are saved of the tribes of Israel, who go through that fiery, furious ordeal of the wrath of men against God's people. He is a type of those Gentiles who go through that burning furnace, that lions' den, and who are saved. And he is a type of the remnant saved in the great tribulation.

The story is, also, a type of what shall happen to the enemies of God. "And the king commanded, and they brought those men which had accused Daniel, and they cast them into the den of lions, them, their children, and their wives; and the lions had the mastery of them, and brake all their bones in pieces or ever they came at the bottom of the den" (Dan. 6:24). There will come a time of judgment upon the wicked. Wickedness and iniquity shall not prevail in the earth forever. There is a day when God shall purge it out and there shall be established a kingdom of righteousness, holiness, godliness, and saintliness. There will come a day when sin is destroyed forever, a day when there is no more death, no more sorrow, no more crying, and no more pain. When sin is cast out and when Satan is cast out, there is also cast out death, suffering, and sorrow. And in the new heaven and in the new earth we will shine in God's kingdom as Daniel shone in incomparable grace and goodness when he was raised out of the den of lions to stand as God's man in the earth.

Help us, Lord, thus to praise Thee and to honor Thee now and forever.